F[redacted]CK
FAILURE

F[redacted]CK FAILURE

benny blanco

SIMON & SCHUSTER

London · New York · Amsterdam/Antwerp · Sydney/Melbourne · Toronto · New Delhi

First published in the United States by Simon & Schuster,
an imprint of Simon & Schuster, LLC, 2026

First published in Great Britain by Simon & Schuster UK Ltd, 2026

1 3 5 7 9 10 8 6 4 2

Simon & Schuster UK Ltd
7th Floor
199 Bishopsgate
London EC2M 3TY

www.simonandschuster.co.uk
www.simonandschuster.com.au
www.simonandschuster.co.in

Simon & Schuster Australia, Sydney
Simon & Schuster India, New Delhi

The authorised representative in the EEA is Simon & Schuster Netherlands BV, Herculesplein 96, 3584 AA Utrecht, Netherlands. info@simonandschuster.nl

A CIP catalogue record for this book is available from the British Library

Hardback ISBN: 978-1-3985-6733-7
Trade Paperback ISBN: 978-1-3985-6846-4
eBook ISBN: 978-1-3985-6734-4

Interior design by Lewelin Polanco

Printed and Bound in the UK using 100% Renewable Electricity at CPI Group (UK) Ltd

FSC www.fsc.org
MIX
Paper | Supporting responsible forestry
FSC® C013604

I want to dedicate this book

to anyone who's doubted me,

thought my dreams wouldn't come true,

or told me no along the way.

Let your actions quiet the noise

until your actions become the noise

everyone's talking about.

Contents

F[redacted]CK FAILURE

You Are a Failure.

All right, you did it. You got this book. You opened it up; you sat down to read it or turned it on in your car to listen to while you picked your nose and thought no one was looking. I saw that.

You came here because you've got places to go. Things to do. A new life to create. A new career to start. Money to make. People to impress. Ideas to launch. A burning feeling in your belly that you know you won't be able to shake until you do something about it. Then you heard that I wrote a book about success, whatever that means. I mean, *I* know what it means;

I wrote the damn book, but let's not get ahead of ourselves. Right now, you're hoping that you can get in on some of that success too. Whatever that might be, you want it. And I want it for you. We're gonna do great things together.

But before we get started, there's something you have to know:

You're a failure.

I mean it. Repeat after me: **I. Am. A. Failure.**

I know those are some of the scariest words that could ever come out of your mouth. But now that you've said them, isn't it a little freeing? Like, what were you so scared of? Letting yourself down? Letting your parents down? Letting some douchebag who works across the hallway from you down?

Chances are extremely high that you are actually a failure at something. Congrats on that—it's officially the most interesting thing about you.

You probably even failed today. Not looking for a new job even though you've been promising yourself you would for months. Hitting the snooze button for your workout this morning. Yelling at your kids when you promised yourself you wouldn't but they wouldn't put on their shoes and get in the fucking car. And now that you've owned up to being a failure and you see that no one's coming for you because of it, we can move on from here.

Our egos make it hard for us to accept not being able to do something we set out to do. We look at failure like it permanently defines us. As if once you fail, you couldn't possibly try that thing you were doing again. Because you could never, ever do *anything* right again.

And forget trying to talk about failure. It's like your parents getting a divorce. Or hair plugs. Or death. No one wants to come out and say, "You know what I did today? I really ate it." But where does that get you besides therapy, or believing that high school was the best years of your life? So we're gonna talk about it. Because if you're gonna get where you want to go—in business, in love, in family, in sports, in art—then you're gonna have to fail first.

You're gonna fail *so many times*. I fail constantly. Songs don't hit as high on the Billboard list as I thought they would; collaborations get weird; people don't love what I've made for them; I forget a friend's birthday. I've had small, everyday failures and *massive* failures. I've had *years* of failure when I wasn't sure if I'd ever work again. And you just bought a book with my name on it, so you can probably guess that it all turned out okay.

Michael Jordan got cut from his high school varsity basketball team, and he's the best basketball player of all time. Unless you think LeBron or Kobe are better, but don't screw up this metaphor for me. Oprah Winfrey was demoted from a prime-time co-anchor role. Sylvester Stallone had to sell his dog for forty dollars outside a 7-Eleven because he was so broke while writing *Rocky*. (He eventually bought him back for fifteen grand.) You think every invention Thomas Edison made was 10/10? I don't really know, but I'm guessing they probably weren't. What were they supposed to do? Cry about it? No. They got up, and they tried again. Eventually, you do that enough times that it works out. Know why? Because those failures are what make success possible.

No one wins right away or all the time. That reality just doesn't exist. We've been sold this really messed-up story that if you don't get something from the jump, you're a failure. And if you're a failure, then you're the worst. But what if, just for a minute, you let yourself see that failure is a part of life. That it's *supposed* to happen. Would we have a single great novel or movie if the main character walked in page one, scene one, did exactly what they were supposed to do and left? No, they have to find their way through the darkest forest and take a wrong turn and get struck by lightning and fight dragons with one arm before they get the money and the girl. And we're there, cheering them on the whole time because we understand on some level that failure is what made the hero stronger. Failure is what gives the journey meaning. Failure is what makes it all awesome.

When I first got the idea to write this book, I wanted to just hand you a sheet of paper that said:

Failure + Failure = Success

My editor told me to go fuck myself.

See, my first failure at this whole book thing, done. But it only would have been a true failure if I'd quit, and *quit* isn't in my vocabulary, so here's fifty thousand more words about it.

Failure doesn't mean "Go home."

No, it's "Success: coming soon."

It's "Keep going."

It's "We'll get 'em next time."

It's "Oh, if I change one thing around, it's gonna work" or "Tomorrow, we're gonna try this again, but maybe go left instead of right."

Failure is one of the most powerful opportunities you'll ever be handed in life. And life doesn't exactly go around handing out opportunities. When you fail, you're getting feedback. It's like someone giving you a play-by-play of what you did wrong and how to do it better the next time. Maybe you need more experience or education. Maybe the idea needs fine-tuning. Maybe not a single thing is wrong, just the timing isn't right. Then you *use* that intel. And you show yourself that there is no limit to what you can do. Because the worst-case scenario of trying anything at all, the complete apocalyptic endgame, is that someone else says no, and you get to come back smarter, stronger, and more determined.

Failure is just another rehearsal for your opening night.

Failure is just more practice for perfection.

And soon enough, failure will start to feel good.

Once you realize that failure is freedom, you'll never look back. You'll realize that you don't have to be embarrassed anymore. Failing is by far not the worst thing that could happen to you. And everyone else is too wrapped up in their own shit and their own failures to really care.

Seriously, if someone in your life is keeping a running list of your failures on a whiteboard in their bedroom, they're a weirdo. Find a new friend.

The only real failure is something that keeps you from trying again. Anything else is just one more shot. It's doing everything you possibly can until there is no other option *but* to succeed.

Take Bruno Mars. I've known him since around 2008, and he is the epitome of not giving up. He's been hustling since he was basically a toddler—you can find clips of him on the internet working as an Elvis impersonator at like three years old. In 2004, he finally got signed to Motown Records. They dropped him the same year. That's not an uncommon story in the music business, but what's special about it is what happened next. After being dropped, he reinvented himself as a producer-songwriter and gets a publishing deal. Eventually, he met his musical soulmate in Philip Lawrence, who at the time was working as Donald Duck or something at Disney World. In 2006, two years after Bruno was dropped, they met the guy who would sign them to Atlantic Records, my friend Aaron Bay-Schuck. But it wasn't so straightforward. It took Aaron *three more years* to convince Atlantic to sign them, because everyone at the label said Bruno wasn't ready. Eventually, Bruno and Philip made demos for "Nothin' on You" by B.o.B. and "Billionaire" by Travie McCoy, which they hoped would help them finally get signed. Initially, an A&R executive at Atlantic wanted to replace Bruno, who was singing on both songs, because he was an unknown artist and this guy thought it would be better to put on someone who was already signed to the label. But Aaron wouldn't give up on Bruno. He played the demos for the chairman of Atlantic, who then decided that not only should they keep Bruno on the songs, but they should sign him—and then use the songs to help break *him* as an artist. The songs became hits, Bruno released his debut single "Just the Way You Are," and he's never looked back since.

It would have been so easy for him to have given up. On paper, it probably would have made more sense for him to move on. But he didn't take no as the final answer—mostly because he knew that at some point, he'd get the only yes he'd ever need. One hundred and eighty million singles, some Grammys, and a Super Bowl say he was right.

Success isn't defined by a Lamborghini and a fancy penthouse apartment. It's the grind. The come-up.

You want success? You gotta fail *better*.

Take it from me, a person who has succeeded, then failed, then succeeded, then failed, then succeeded again. I've learned a few tricks along the way. And all of them have to do with turning fucking up into an art form. So even though, technically, there are no shortcuts to success . . . there kinda are. Because if you're nailing the fail part, success is gonna follow.

I'm not one of those bullshit motivational speakers who's just gonna give you some big abstract ideas to believe in, then take my publishing advance to the bank while you figure the rest out. What I *am* going to give you are actual tools that you can use in your own life. Tools that don't require you to go anywhere or buy anything. Tools based on real stories and real problems I've had—and that some of my friends have had. How we got into them, and how we found our way out. And how that led me here. "Here" being a New York City apartment overlooking Central Park, realizing that there are way too many people walking around so terrified of failing that they'll never, ever do anything that sets them up to actually succeed. And I can't have that.

My job as a collaborator and a producer—like, my actual job—is to pull success out of someone. When an artist comes to me, it's because they're missing the perfect song or a piece of their album. For whatever reason, they're stuck. Maybe on some level they feel like a failure. And they know that, no matter what, I'm going to help them get *un*stuck. But it's not because my superpower is cranking out hit songs. My superpower is helping people tap into the success that's already inside of them. Sure, I can offer a swig of the magic potion that gives people everything they walked in wanting in the first place, but at the end of the day, it's all them. And always has been.

One time I was working on a song with Ed Sheeran. It started out like any other session. Except usually when we write together, Ed is touching on his own experience. But in this case, he was trying to tell a story about sleeping with a MILF inspired by *The Graduate*—not something pulled from his own life. I immediately paused what we were doing and said, "What's going on? Why aren't we writing about something real?" We listened to the playback, and he was like, "Yeah, you're right; this sucks." I said, "Well, what's going on in your life? Why can't we just write about that like we always do?" And he said, "I broke up with a girl, and I don't want to give her the satisfaction of knowing that I'm thinking about her all the time, enough to write a full song about it." To which I said, "So let's write a song about *that*."

And I didn't wanna write a song
'Cause I didn't want anyone thinking I still care

Those were the first lyrics we put down for what eventually became Justin Bieber's "Love Yourself."

This will sound like the cheesiest bullshit, but I promise you it's not: Everyone can be successful. *I* know it. But *you* have to know it.

If you don't plan on reading any more of this book, do me one favor: Remember that table of contents a few pages back? I want you to rip it out and put it in your pocket. Or if you're going to lose that, roll it up and tuck it in your tushy for later.

These are the non-shortcut shortcuts to success:

1. **Shut up.** So many people are going to shit on your dreams on your way to success. Don't be one of them.

2. **Dream big.** Like BIG. Let's make a beautiful mess.
3. **Live like it's real.** Nothing to see here but hard work. I never said it was gonna be easy. Get strategic, make a plan—but never a plan B.
4. **Fail until it feels good.** Crash, burn, repeat, and never, ever quit.
5. **Don't be a dick.** Conflict is a waste of energy and the best idea wins, period.
6. **Be nice to yourself.** You only have one chance at this life, and you're kinda all you got.
7. **Relax.** Let it ride. There's always tomorrow.

That's it. Those are the steps. The rules. The commandments. Whatever you want to call them.

It doesn't matter what you did yesterday, this morning, an hour ago—if you want to make a difference in your life, this is how to live *now*. It's what made me successful in all aspects of my life. It's what taught me how to go after the absurdly big dreams that I've had since I was a kid and to never accept less. It's what helped me survive in a cutthroat industry without being a scumbag. It's what gave me patience. It's what helped me understand my partner and give her what she wants and needs, while also getting what I want and need. It's what helped me process a complicated relationship with my dad. It's what helped me become best friends with my mom. It's what helped me show up better for myself. All these things, to me, are success in every sense of the word. And it comes down to these seven ideas.

If you let it, this book can change your life. But I want you to know something: Even after you've read it five times, even after all of your dreams have come true, even after you start climbing that next mountain . . .

You are still going to be a failure.

And that's great.

c[redacted]er

1

Shut Up.

All this talk of success probably has you getting a little foamy at the corners of your mouth. You're counting all the ways you're about to level up. All those New Year's resolutions you're finally gonna make good on. That vision board that you made at the bachelorette party with the rose gold Bentley and a golden retriever will finally come to life.

That's great. You know I'm here to make your dreams come true. But what would you do if I told you to put this book down and first go tackle one pivotal thing that will change your life forever? Seriously, go. I'll wait.

Ah, you're still here. Thank you for proving my point. I got a little nervous about that gamble.

My guess is that when I tell you to go, right fucking now, do one thing that you *know* would make your life better and happier and full of all the stuff you want—you freeze. You doubt. You talk yourself out of it. You make excuses. There's probably a reallllly good one you've been milking for all its worth.

I don't have the right education.
I don't have the right experience.
I don't have the right body type.
I don't have the time.
It's not the right *time.*
I'm too old.
I'm too young.
There's already someone out there doing what I want to do.
I'm tired.

No really, I'm exhausted just from making that list.

Look, I'm not judging you. I can't expect that telling you fifty times over the course of fifteen pages that failure is cool and necessary will be enough to change your mind. I mean, for the sake of being done with writing this book, I wish it was. But I know it's not. And that's fair.

So let's try this another way: You're standing at the starting line. You're about to go on this epic adventure that is *guaranteed* to take you somewhere other than where you are right now. In the best possible way. The only thing you need to do right now? Shut up.

Seriously, shut the fuck up. Turn off the voices in your head telling you, *No, we shouldn't do that.* I don't care if you don't think you're good enough yet at what you want to do. I don't care if you've never done it before. I don't care if you think your time has passed. Bill Withers was thirty-three when he started making music. Julia Child was forty-nine when she published her first cookbook and in her fifties when she filmed her show. Harland Sanders founded KFC at sixty-two. There isn't one thing that you can tell me, not one excuse you can list, that could possibly make me say to you, "Okay, fine, your dreams are dumb." So why are you telling yourself that?

When you're a kid and you have a dream, you just have that dream. If you decide you want to be an astronaut, your next thought isn't, *Well, but I have allergies and my nose is gonna get all runny in my helmet and I'm actually a little claustrophobic and I'm not the best at math.*

No, you're imagining yourself flying through the Earth's atmosphere and seeing stars and floating outside in space and that's the end of my examples because I didn't dream about becoming an astronaut. The point being, you gave yourself permission to have these big goals based on nothing other than the fact that they sounded cool or fun. And, in your own five-year-old way, you'd chase them with zero hesitation or regrets.

That's what I need you to do now. Because a dream only stays a dream if you don't put it in motion.

The most important thing you can realize is that until you ignore those voices saying that you *can't* get there eventually, none of this is going to work. And that *is* failing. The bad kind. So what other reason do you have left not to try?

None.

The best advice I ever got about irrational fears of failing came from my therapist, Dr. Barry Lubetkin. I would talk to him, for hours, about my intense fear of crashing to my death in an airplane. It's my number one fear. To the point where, to this day, I would rather pack up all my stuff and take four days to drive cross-country in a tour bus just to get between Los Angeles and New York or take a boat between the United States and Europe than get on a plane for a few hours. Because back in 2009, just hours after Sully landed his plane in the Hudson River, I got on a flight from New York to Atlanta where the turbulence was so bad that even the flight attendants looked like they were done for. At one point one of them accidentally pressed the intercom button when asking the pilot, "Are we going to be okay?" We got to Atlanta, but then I had to get on this tiny ten-seater that was taking me to Panama City, Florida, and for the entire hour-long flight, we were tossed around in this crazy lightning storm. I took a cross-country train home. That experience stirred up some deep-seated neuroses/control issues/existential dread that I fell deeper and deeper into. I attempted to fly every now and then, until, while I was on a flight to London to see my at-the-time girlfriend, we hit a huge turbulence surge and my television screen broke off the hinge connecting it to my arm rest, and I promised myself I'd never fly again. It's the one thing I can't crush. I'd never tell you I was perfect; I wouldn't trust anyone who is. So for me, that's my thing. The one failure I'm still trying to take my own advice on.

During one session, my therapist said to me: "Do you think you're so important that God is going to take time out of His busy schedule to make sure that you fall out of the sky and take down 150 other people with you? You're not that special."

Damn.

What he meant was that we all think we're some kind of exception to the rule. Or that our circumstances are somehow different from everyone else's. Is flying a perfectly safe and trusted mode of transportation for millions of people every single day? Of course. Is there a non-zero chance that something bad could happen? Sure. But what is it about me or you that would make that an even bigger probability? Absolutely nothing.

There's not one thing about you in particular that makes failure more likely. It feels good to believe that there is. A little *too* good. Because if you're dead set on the idea that you'll always fail, then you never have to try. Right? What's the point?

That's the saddest, most depressing reality you could ever make for yourself. If you're here to make things happen in your life, the fastest way to set that on fire is to believe you're screwed from the jump. It's another voice in your head that needs to be left on read.

Maybe you're worried that everyone's out there watching your every move like when you were in middle school and got a pimple on your nose and thought it was going to be announced over the loudspeaker. Yeah, maybe some asshole made fun of you for it, but it's more likely that everyone was too busy worrying about the pimples on their own noses.

Think about what you could get done if you thought more about the very real things that you have the unique ability to do versus what you're *imagining* people think you can't. No one cares, because you're not that special. Doesn't that feel kind of great?

Right now you're standing at the starting line I just told you about. The one where just a single step forward is moving you closer to everything you want your life to be. It's gonna take a bunch more steps to get there, and there's gonna be all kinds of nonsense that comes up along the way—and we'll deal with that. But right now, that first step is all you have to worry about.

So do me a favor, shut up, and do it. I love you.

c[redacted]er

2

Dream Big.

One night when I was five years old, I ran out of my bedroom, naked, holding a portable CD player in one hand and a speaker in the other, dancing and screaming the words to Prince's "Sexy MF." I got to the end of the hallway, huffing and puffing, looked up, and saw my mother and all her friends in the middle of a dinner party. I stared her right in the eyes and said, "I'm gonna be the biggest artist in the world." Then I ran away.

That was *my* astronaut dream. While other kids were in their Superman pajamas, lying in their bunk beds imagining themselves fighting bad guys or putting out fires or eating mountains of Jell-O, I was dreaming about music. Listening to it, making it, being around it. I didn't know any of the particulars. I didn't have some kind of plan to get a degree in musical theory or take lessons or apprentice with a professional. I was five. But from as early as I could remember, I knew that music would be a part of my life. I would go to the record store with my big brother, Jeremy, almost every day. I would study the liner notes of the albums before I could even read and listen to all the tapes my parents would let me buy, starting with Nas's "The World Is Yours" and All-4-One's "I Swear." I became obsessed.

At thirteen, instead of hanging out with my friends during lunch, I'd be in the Langston Hughes Middle School library, logging into my Myspace account and writing every record label and every person in the music industry whose information I could find online. There wasn't anyone in Reston, Virginia, who could help me, so I had to make my world bigger. Social media meant that there was a chance that I could reach out to someone and they'd actually write me back. It made my dream feel tangible, even though my friends couldn't understand why I wanted more for myself than Snack Packs and kickball, or how I felt like I already knew everything I needed to know from school—and that I was ready for the next step of my life. So I sent hundreds of messages a day to producers, artists, label execs. If I did happen to get a meeting—which was usually canceled after I'd already driven the four and a half hours to New York City in my friend's car—I'd camp out at the twenty-four-hour McDonald's in Times Square, wake up the next day, and start all over again.

One time I looked up which record label Jay-Z was signed to so I could cold call the label president. I told the assistant that I was Jay-Z's attorney Michael Guido and that I needed to talk about Jay-Z's contract *right now*. She said, "Right away, sir," and patched me through. When the label president picked up, I said, "This isn't Michael Guido—but don't hang up! My name is benny blanco, and I have the best demo you have ever heard."

Click.

It's been like this for me my whole life, down to my love of running around with no pants on. I've always had big dreams, like I came out of the womb with some kind of assassin's list of what I was going to accomplish.

I also experienced a decent amount of adversity to those dreams throughout my life, but particularly as a kid. I'm not gonna spend too much time wallowing in that fact because that adversity became fuel and not a setback, but basically, I had to grow up quickly.

My dad struggled with his mental health. He also felt more connected to my brother, the athletic, popular golden child.

They had a macho synergy and bonded over basketball and my brother wanting to be a professional tennis player.

My mom, on the other hand, doesn't have a mean bone in her body. She does, however, have a fear of nearly everything, including following her dreams. She would give me a million excuses about why she stopped painting or modeling and instead worked a string of mundane, soulless jobs.

As a child, she was told she couldn't dream. That she wasn't good enough to dream. A worrier raised her. I don't know much about my family tree, but I'm sure her mother's mother was a worrier, too. And my mom raised me with that anxiety. *What's your backup plan? Why don't you get a college degree? There's a one-in-a-billion chance that you could ever make it in the music industry!* I'd be fourteen, fifteen years old, already traveling around the country, running recording studio rooms with grown adults, and I'd see her pulling studio people aside to—not entirely unreasonably—ask, "Is he even that good?" And somehow that voice didn't end up becoming my own voice. It creeps in from time to time—I can't pretend it doesn't, and we'll talk about what I do when it does—but I know that it's not my voice that I'm hearing. It's someone else's generations-old worry, and it's not meant for me.

People hear my story and want to believe that my success is a result of me trying to prove that I'm good enough. That I wanted to be the golden child. But here's the thing: The voices in my head have never been negative. I'm serious. It has only been *GO* my entire life. A will and a drive where you can't stop me unless you kill me. I had no other choice *but* to succeed because I wanted it so much as a kid. I didn't want to know what a world would look like if I didn't get that. It wasn't a question of whether I would make it, but whether anyone would see this underdog coming. My obstacles made me hungrier.

My dad, who could sell a ketchup Popsicle to a lady in a wedding dress, taught me the gift of gab, how to light up a room, and how to have confidence no matter how big a swing I was taking.

My mom might not have gone after her childhood dreams, but she eventually found new dreams—to be a great mother, and eventually, a great-grandmother—and she's killing it. Her unconditional love with a heavy sprinkling of neuroses helped shape me into who I am today. She taught me to be open to any path or relationship. To jump at every opportunity, no matter how high it might be, and to not be afraid of the fall on the way down. She never spoiled me, but she always made sure I knew my worth. She taught me that I was a catch. That I had important things to say. Even if she didn't always understand or believe in the things I did. She told me how good I was and that I could do whatever I set my mind to. So even though my mom was too scared to do any of these things herself, she provided a safety net so that if I fell fifty thousand feet, I would land in one of those gymnastics foam pits that smell weird and will give you pink eye if you're not careful.

All of the above went into making sure that my big dreams

stayed really freaking big. Bigger than they had any right to be. Look at me, I'm like a cross between André the Giant and Danny DeVito. I'm five-foot-five on a good day. I grew up in a tiny condominium in a place that nobody left and where nobody had any connections. I was hyperactive. I couldn't sit still in class; I talked too much; and when they tried to separate me from the other kids, I'd just sing to myself. I was diagnosed with ADHD and OCD. I didn't do well with authority figures. I knew that school wasn't going to get me where I wanted to go, so I just wanted to do what I wanted to do, when I wanted to do it. If I wasn't skipping class to hang out with my friends, I was skipping class to sneak into the band room to make music. I thought I was being proactive. School didn't see it that way. I embarrassed my mom. I never did end up being able to read music or play an instrument very well. Most of the riffs for my early songs are only two notes because of that. I'm also not very good with electronics. At some point I didn't even know you could change the grid type on Pro Tools to adjust the tempo, which is why all my first big songs are 120 bpm. I'm the pure definition of willing something into existence. And yet somehow, I became a person who makes Billboard number ones; who is married to the nicest, smartest, most beautiful person on planet Earth; and whose life is full of things I love to do. The world is my oyster and I made sure it came with a side of lemon, Crystal hot sauce, and a little caviar.

Let's order a couple dozen for you too.

This is where I tell you that you can be and do whatever

you want. I get that it might be a tough idea to wrap your head around. We're taught to not follow our dreams, that there's only one "normal" path, or that there's only one winner. Lucky for you, I've called bullshit on that from the jump.

You might not know yet what you want most in your life—and that's okay; we're getting there. But the only way you're going to be able to take that thing once you do figure it out, lasso it, have your way with it, and ride it into the sunset is if you start thinking a lot bigger about what you want. Maybe even to the point that it makes you feel a little uncomfortable. A little ridiculous. A little nervous. Let me know when you're flat-out ready to shit your pants. Because that's when we take the next step. I'll just be waiting over here as your safety net so that you can take those same leaps fifty thousand feet into the air and know you'll be okay.

What Even Is Success?

I know I've gotten you all worked up about diving in *right fucking now* and starting your new successful life—and I still want you to do that—but first I want to talk about what, exactly, success is. Because how else will you know where you're going?

Success looks different for everyone. This isn't a handbook to become the next Mark Cuban. No disrespect to Mark Cuban, but I don't want to be him. And I don't want you to be him. I want you to be [INSERT YOUR FIRST AND LAST NAME]—and yes, all caps because you're the shit now. This also isn't a handbook to prove your mom or dad wrong. You might want to get a different book for that.

Success isn't just chasing one thing. It's what a bunch of things add up to. It isn't necessarily breaking every Billboard record that exists or running a Fortune 500 company that just had a $4 billion acquisition. For me, it's getting to do the things I love on a daily basis, being challenged and pushed and stressed and frustrated and totally content. Knowing that I created this world where I get to work hard as shit all day then come home and chill with my partner and eat snacks on a couch while watching a movie with my hands down my pants. Sleeping like a rock, then waking up, alive to see another day in a body that still works, next to my beautiful wife, who, out of every single person on planet Earth, was stupid enough to pick me. Getting to have conversations with friends that make me laugh and cry and think.

I can't forget about my dogs—they're success. Because their lives are perfect. They just get to wake up long enough to eat, shit wherever they want, and play. Who knows, maybe a dog doesn't think their life is success. But to me, a dog is success.

Those are all the same type of victory. Success is owning your life. Doing your best to plan while God laughs, holding on like you're trying to hit eight seconds on the rodeo bull, and maybe even steering a little.

My guess is you've already achieved some kind of success and that you don't give it the recognition that it deserves. It isn't always a fancy car in your driveway. It might be the job that covers your bills with enough left over to buy a few things that make you happy. It might be having the flexibility to travel, or to work from your bed. It might be your child who you get to raise differently than you were raised. Or maybe it *is* the fancy car in your driveway, and that's okay. Just don't be a dick about it.

And here you are, wanting more. I get that. The most successful people never fully succeed because they're always on to the next thing. It's always like success, *question mark*? As long as you can look at your life, see the good stuff for what it is, *and* want more, then I'm in favor of that question mark.

Me, no matter how good life gets—maybe even because of how good life gets—I'm always chasing that question of what's next or how can I do what I'm doing, only better. I have OCD—when I walk into a room, a room that most people might see as totally fine, I see all these things that I have to fix and straighten and put in order. That pack of gum on the table should be horizontal instead of vertical so you can read the label. The pair of shoes you take off by my front door should be lined up straight against the wall, or, better yet, in the corner so they're flush against the wall on two sides. The chairs at the dining room table should either all be pushed in or left a foot or two out, but not both (someone please tell my wife this). That might not be other people's sense of perfect, but it's mine. And while I've made peace with some of the stuff that I cannot control—because you can't successfully live life otherwise—these are my things.

I see the world the same way. I'm constantly out there thinking, *Oooh, I can make that straight.* Meaning, I can do that little extra bit that makes it my kind of *perfect.* Working and working and working on a song until everything's nestled just right. Rolling that song out in just the right way so we can leave a little Easter egg for later, coordinating my outfit so it matches a set. Basically, it's never settling when you know you could do better. I hear people say all the time, "That's the best I could do"—but I don't know if it is. It's like when you're at the gym you tell your trainer or your friend that you couldn't do any more reps and they say, "Yes, you can," and you're like, "No, I physically can't," and then you do fifteen more and are like, *Where did that come from?*

Success is when you're willing to find that out.

Success is curiosity, the drive to discover. It's when one voice in the back of my head goes, *You did it, man,* after hitting one goal, then another voice from the other side of my head goes, *Now what are we gonna go fuck up?* And drives me to find success in something else—maybe that's in my professional life, or maybe it's something else I'm passionate about, like collecting art or fly fishing. Maybe it's how I show up in relationships. Success is beating the game, then realizing the game has infinite levels.

Success is defined by a goal that you set that you work so unbelievably hard at and then accomplish. But maybe, above everything else, it's the knowing that you did it. And that it made you feel happy. Or fulfilled. Even if the outcome looks different than what you originally had in mind. The money and the other cool stuff may just show up, but knowing what success looks like to you and what you want so damn bad has to come first.

Let's go get you some big, juicy goals.

Make a Mess

In 2017, the documentary series *The Defiant Ones* had just come out. It's about Jimmy Iovine and Dr. Dre and how they came from these vastly different worlds and against all odds transformed music and culture. Around that time, I was with Ed Sheeran in Boston, where he was on tour and we were working on his third album, ÷. We started the series one morning, and Ed was so amped about it that after his show at Gillette Stadium that night, he had a car waiting for us so he could literally run offstage and go back to his hotel room to keep watching. Thinking this way about this work we do is all about made a pretty big impact on us, to the point where the next night, when we were back at the stadium waiting for him to go on and finally finished the last episode, Ed immediately stands up and goes, "What the fuck are we doing with our lives?"

At that exact moment, the tour manager comes in to give Ed the five-minute warning. He got dressed, then went upstairs to play to eighty thousand people.

I, meanwhile, am still sitting downstairs alone, hugging a giant teddy bear, continuing to wonder, *What the fuck* am *I doing with my life?*

At that point, I had been writing and producing songs for other people for about ten years. It was strange because I could see what a huge success that was, but I was also getting tired of doing the exact same thing over and over again. I know that's playing the world's smallest violin for myself, but it was like living in the twilight zone—my days were all running together. I'd wake up, go into the studio, and make songs for someone else. I was just doing the thing. And it wasn't giving me the same feeling, the same joy it once did. I missed being challenged. I missed waking up in the morning, stepping in some shit and figuring my way out of it—the way I'd always done it. I missed the hunger for making things work and the nausea of not knowing when the pieces were going to come together, or if they ever were. I missed the mess.

I had gotten comfortable writing songs and giving them to people who I thought were better than me. The way I saw it, there were people who are born to be performers, and I wasn't one of them. I figured I was meant to be in the background as a fixer and a therapist, listening and helping someone else through their journey. That made me feel good about myself, but I wasn't getting the same high anymore.

I thought about how Dr. Dre had so much success after he founded his record label, but also how things really jelled when he started putting out his new music. And what I realized in this *What the fuck*? moment was that I didn't want to only make music for other people anymore. I wanted to make music for me. As an artist.

When you write a song for someone, you don't have any say in what happens once it's finished. That artist decides how the promotions are going to go, how the video rollouts are going to go, how the marketing is going to go. That's their choice and what they're supposed to do, and for a really long time, I didn't mind that. I didn't need more from that process. But now here I was, sitting there thinking, *I bet I could make a whole album that represents me as an artist. I bet I could make a cool video. I bet I could come up with some cool marketing. So what am I waiting for? We're all gonna die—why not at least try?* And where I wanted to start was with the demo I'd just written with Ed in a hotel room back in Philadelphia.

Ed came back after the show. And here's the thing about Ed: He can walk in after playing for two hours to tens of thousands of people and pick up the conversation exactly where he left off.

I said, "Dude, I think I want to be an artist, and I think I want to use the demo as one of my first songs." I was terrified. I thought he'd tell me to shut up because he was putting it on his own album. But all he said was:

"Yeah, that'd be cool." He was genuinely surprised I hadn't done it sooner.

Shit.

I was kind of hoping he'd say no.

But he said yes. So I made an album and I put that song out, which became "Eastside" with Halsey and Khalid. I had no idea it would be the success that it was—frankly, I was the last person to see that it had the potential to blow up. All I knew was that I was having fun and feeling totally fulfilled, like I was eighteen again and making music just for me.

Most of us are really good at holding onto this idea of what we *think* we're supposed to do. We worry about what's gonna happen if we take a step off the path—even if that path is one we chose, like, decades ago. Think of the movie *Finding Nemo*. Nemo was living the same life, the same *day*, over and over again. But he knew that there was something bigger out there. Now, I don't think Nemo was thinking in terms of success—he was a fish—but I do think we all have a little Nemo in us, just like we all have Nemo's dad following us around and telling us what we're supposed to do and what's *safe*. It feels kinda scary to ask yourself, *Is there something else out there that I really wish I could be doing?* But the answer is usually yes. And I don't know about you, but I think it's a whole lot scarier to think I could die tomorrow with that regret.

When I decided to become an artist, I told myself I would make a huge record. Maybe it wouldn't be the very first one, but eventually. Then "Eastside" came out. And there it was, the huge record.

I had to ask myself again, *Well, now what*? And think of a new thing. Find a new way to challenge myself. Make a new mess. So I decided to write a cookbook. In what world do I get to write a cookbook? I'm not a professional chef. Or in what world will it succeed to the point where I get to be a *New York Times* bestselling author? In what world do I get to be on a television show? For every single one of these sort of bucket-list things, I just closed my eyes, said, "Fuck it," and jumped into the deep end.

Every New Year's Eve, I say to my team, "Let's make a mess." What I mean by that is, *Let's throw a bunch of crazy stuff at the wall and see what sticks.* It's a list of all the things I want to achieve the following year, from starting a record label to eating more fruit. And both of those things are equally important to me. You might argue that the fruit is even more important than the record label, but I don't know how soft your stool is.

Some things on the list are laser-focused, like walking twenty thousand steps a day instead of fifteen thousand. Or not forgetting to brush my teeth before I go to bed. Others are a little bit more abstract, like reinventing the podcast industry or opening a bed-and-breakfast whose proceeds go toward helping people experiencing food insecurity. And there are usually between twenty and fifty things on there. Want to know what my list looks like right now, as I'm typing?

Finish this book.

Write and develop a limited series TV show. Maybe a movie too.

Launch a TV/film production company and marketing company.

Write two albums.

Pre-record podcast episodes for next year's launch.

Write another cookbook. This time with my wife.

How do I get all that done in the time I have in the day/week/year? I don't know. But I'm going to figure it out, because I'm always going to back myself into a corner and fight my way out. That's always how it's been for me. So that's the rule: Once it's on the list, it has to happen. There's no going back. It is written.

I don't necessarily have to know how or when each thing is going to happen. Some things stay on the list for years; others fall off January 2. Like remembering to brush my teeth. Both are huge wins. Because I didn't stop until I got it all done.

Why do I do it? Because it feels so good to live in the mess. Like I have no idea what I'm doing—because most of the time, I really don't. Once I get an idea for a song, I can usually hear it as a whole and see what it's going to become right away, but I don't know how I'm going to get there. Sometimes I'm starting with just a title. Or a riff in my head. Or maybe some chords. Sometimes I'll have an experience, and I'll want to use that. Sometimes I'm just going for a vibe. Or I'll hear a sound that I like. Or I'll play an instrument that inspires me because it's old or weird-sounding or just gives me some kind of feeling. And then I have to commit to the process of somehow turning that into a song, which means pretty much letting things go where they're going to go until I have something I'm satisfied with, then reworking it and reworking it and reworking it until I can sleep at night knowing it's the best it can possibly be. That's as close to a science as it gets.

Here's a great example: I'm at the gym with my brother in 2009. At this point in my life I never worked out, but for whatever reason, there I was on the treadmill. All of a sudden, I start hearing this riff in my head. I didn't have my phone with me so I grab Jeremy's, and, still trying to catch my breath, record this little melody-thing. *Da da duh duh, da duh duh duh duh.* I get to the studio the next morning way before anyone else is there for the day. I'm not very good with technology and the synthesizers weren't plugged in yet, so the only thing I can get to record is a grand piano. I record the opening riff for what would eventually become Taio Cruz's "Dynamite." Then I start playing around with chopping it up and really compressing it using the one compressor in the studio that was working, which I also didn't really know how to use. It ended up making this really interesting sound, which I put some drums on. Eventually everyone else gets there and is like, *Whoa, this sounds crazy,* and we all start trying different things and adding different elements. Max Martin, who is on a beach somewhere, puts down a little bit of the chorus: *I throw my hands up in the air sometimes / Sayin' "Ayo, gotta let go."* Then I get in the booth and start rap-singing, but it's still missing the melody. Max and Dr. Luke add that melody, including that final little flourish on "dy-na-mite."

Then the song sat. For months. Mainly because it was a mess—it had me singing, Max singing. So then Luke rerecorded the whole chorus as one voice. And then Taio Cruz got ahold of it and recorded his own version. Then we wanted to record him on it ourselves because that's what we do, but he was in London and there was a volcano eruption in Iceland that had grounded all the planes, so he took a helicopter to Sweden and recorded it with Max. And then we were all desperately trying to finish it because Taio wanted to put out the song as his next single, which he did. A week later.

Which is all to say, I've never made two songs the same way. Because I couldn't do it any other way than how it had to be done. People always ask me things like, "What were you eating when you recorded X song"—as if they could just be eating that thing too then they'd have a hit. It's not like that. If I knew how to replicate that every time, I promise you every single song I made would be perfect. And a huge success. But as much as I sometimes wish that songwriting was easier, for me, creating is like a drug. There is no substance on this planet that can get me higher than making something. It's this sensation I get deep in my chest, almost like I'm about to kiss someone for the first time. Like *Holy shit I don't know where this is gonna go, but I love it.* I love the chaos of all these things I get to go chase. I love the pressure. Like I barely have any air left in my lungs. I love the roller coaster of *I don't know if I'm going to make it—huh, I am doing it, though, aren't I?* I love the feeling of not knowing the ending of the story. Of never forgetting the hunger that I felt in my bedroom when I was just a kid, dreaming so hard about making it in music that it hurt.

Why don't we go find some things that make you feel that way?

So What's It Gonna Be?

I want you to get a piece of paper and a pen. Or open the notes app on your phone.

Make a list of all the things you want to make better in your life. For real—this is the fun part. You're six years old and the teacher just called on you—what do you want to be when you grow up? What's the first thing that comes to your mind? It can be anything! No one's judging you. It's just you and me here. What are the things you've wished for in the back of your mind but don't let anybody know about because they scare you a little bit? Because if you went for those things, they might totally change the status quo of your life and everything you once thought to be true about yourself. That's the kind of stuff I'm talking about. That's the mess.

What are the things that keep you up at 3 a.m. with your

mind racing because you know, deep down, that you'll never be satisfied until you try them?

What does your perfect day look like? What does your perfect *life* look like? What are you doing? Who are you with? Where are you? How do you feel?

What would make you want to do a somersault out of bed and feel like you have purpose and are working toward something meaningful?

Where do you want to be next year?

In five years?

Seriously, go do it. I'll shut up for a second. And I won't peek.

If you're not as big of a fan of lists as I am, this might sound dumb, like homework. But what's so great about it is that you're not just tossing out a bunch of random stuff into thin air. These are real, concrete things that you can look at every day. When you know what your goals are, you can't pretend that they don't exist anymore.

Just do me one favor: Please don't write, *Being rich and famous*. That's missing the point. Yeah, sure, being rich and famous is cool, but that's not a goal. It should be the by-product of doing something that you love and can't live without, not the actual thing you can't live without.

We're here to figure out what that thing is. Hopefully you just listed a bunch of them. Maybe right now you don't know how they'll make you money—and they might never—but if they're something you're passionate about, then who knows where they could take you? Your goal of having more fresh flowers around the house because they make you feel good might lead you to plant a few small pots on your windowsill. Then maybe one day that'll become a whole bed you build in your backyard. Or in other people's yards. Maybe you start making little arrangements that make you happy. Then you start making arrangements that make other people happy. Until one day that little flowerpot dream becomes the best flower shop or floral design firm in town. And maybe you post about it on social media and find a whole bunch of people who are just as passionate about flowers and plants as you are. You didn't necessarily start out with the goal of any of this bringing you money or fame, but if you listen to that little itch of what you love, it might just do that.

This list is your life-changer. It's what you're going to think about every day. It's going to give you direction. It's going to build character. It's going to make you stronger. It's going to show you that you can do whatever you set your mind to. It's your Philadelphia Museum of Art *Rocky* montage moment. And yeah, things are going to get messy. There are going to be detours. Secret exits. Trapdoors. Side quests. That's the whole point.

Okay, time's up on that list. You good? Great. Now I want you to open an email. Write down all the reasons you *shouldn't* work toward any of the things you just wrote. Make the subject of the email "Why I Shouldn't Follow My Dreams" and send it to bennysaysshutthefuckup@gofuckyourself.com.

You're not done yet, though. My book, my rules.

Before I can set you loose on this Ultimate List of Dreams, we need to make sure that your to-do list is truly setting you up for success. As in, does it have all the major food groups for happiness? Because without that, there is no winning.

Build Your Stool

I want you to take out another piece of paper. Sorry, I should have told you to get two pieces of paper, my bad. Or just invest in a whole fucking journal at this point because I love lists and this isn't going to be the last one you make.

Write down the three most important things in your life. Quick. Don't overthink it.

Unless you're a total psychopath, I can pretty much guarantee your list falls into each of these three categories:

1. Something about relationships (family, friends, pets, etc.)
2. Something about career
3. Something about yourself (health, hobbies, etc.)

These are legitimately the most important things in our lives. Which is why you can't have success in only one of the areas and still succeed at life.

You could prioritize your relationships, but putting everyone else ahead of yourself and your ability to make a living is the definition of toxic boundary issues. You could double down on yourself, but if it's at the expense of the other people in your life and your job, that would be a narcissistic nightmare. And then there's going all in on your career, which is what so many of us fall into the trap of doing and what I did for the first nineteen years of my life. It didn't end well.

My first definition of success was being number one by any means necessary. I'd been that way my entire life, with this unwillingness to quit or lose. Almost like it was a game. But then it happened. In 2008 or 2009 I was sitting in [insert shitty New York nightclub with bottle service] while everyone partied around me, going nuts over a song that had hit number one, a song that I can't even remember at this point, and it was like slow motion because all I could think was, *Why would I stop to celebrate this when I could just go try to do it again?* That's the way it went for years. There was no elation or joy in success; it was just, *Oooh, I want another one.* And, *Oooh, I want another one.* And, *Oooh, I want five.* Pretty quickly, I was investing all this time into my career and I wasn't having the fun I should have been having with my friends. I was neglecting personal relationships. I was neglecting my family. I was neglecting myself, eating pizza and fried chicken strips for every meal. I was pushing my body to the absolute limit, staying up for days because nothing else mattered as much as that song. I wasn't living for anything else besides my work. At one point I was hospitalized for exhaustion. The doctor had to literally prescribe sleep. To the point where people at the studio would be like, "All right benny, it's your curfew; you gotta go home now." And that worked . . . for a little while. Until I figured out that that wasn't success to me. How did I figure it out? Well, the nervous breakdown outside the T-Mobile store at Nineteenth and Broadway when I was twenty years old was a good indicator, but that's another story for another chapter.

When you listen to the world's definition of success, or you only focus on career, money, and being the best, you're going to burn out. You're going to feel isolated. You're going to lose all sense of what this one too-short life is all about and everything that really matters. Trust me.

I know a lot of "successful" people who wake up and all of a sudden, they're fifty. They can rattle off every single thing you might have on your dream list as one of their accomplishments. They have the houses, the cars, the trips, the fuck-you money. But their lives are empty. They're sad and lonely.

I'll be out to dinner with them and all they can talk about is what work project they have coming up next or what they've just finished. They don't have interests outside of what they get paid to do. They don't talk about their family, mostly because a lot of times they don't have a partner or a relationship with their kids; and there's nothing about any friendships outside of people who either work for them, want to work for them, or need something from them.

To anyone looking in from the outside, their lives look amazing. They've made contributions to culture, changed the conversation about things like music and art and movies, made a name for themselves that people will remember—at least for a little while. I want to shake them and scream, "What is the fucking point?!" But then I wouldn't get invited out to very many dinners.

So I'm shaking you instead. There's no such thing as cruising altitude. There's inevitable highs and lows. I've been nominated for Grammys, and I've been on the phone with my manager, crying because of cold streaks that made it feel like I had no choice but to pack it up and move on to the next thing. One day, you're not going to be as good at what you do as you once were. Or at the very least someone will be better than you. And probably younger. And better looking. Or technology is going to change and make you obsolete. Or maybe there won't be so much drama, but you're gonna want to retire. If all your self-worth comes from your career, then who are you when it goes away?

You need an insurance policy. A way to make sure that at every step of this make-life-bigger/better/more satisfying process, you're not losing touch with the things that matter. That policy is those three categories.

Think of them like the legs of a little three-legged stool. The kind that's nice and sturdy and looks like you could make it yourself but furniture stores will try to sell to you for like two thousand dollars. Those legs are, respectively, Relationships, Career, and Self. Then, on top, where your tush goes, is Success.

If you make one of those legs shorter or not as strong as the others, that stool is gonna get wobbly. Take one of the legs away altogether, and you're shit outta luck. And a stool.

The takeaway? **You can't be successful in one area of your life until you're successful in *all* of them.**

This book isn't about becoming the Wolf of Wall Street. I'm not trying to raise the next generation of Patrick Batemans. Sexy? Yes. More murder than we're going for? Also yes. This book is about making your *life* rich.

Every chapter that comes after this one is going to guarantee that. Want to know how I know? Because every single thing I've written about comes from my own experience. Believe me, I'm not smart enough to make it up from scratch. The lessons from here on out are what helped me channel my ambition and passion into a prosperous career, and then helped me put myself back together when I tried to make a mutant stool out of three Career legs. They've helped me pump up the Relationship leg when it was puny and weak from not knowing how I deserved to be treated by others, and they've helped me create daily practices so that the Self leg is a true reflection of everything I need to withstand the crushing blow of any giant ass that tries to sit on my stool. But the biggest win is that now I have this perfect place to rest my own little tuchus when I'm not out there hustling for the work I love with the people I love for a life I love.

Now I want you to go back to the original list you made a chapter ago, the one with all the things you want to succeed at. Look it over again and ask yourself, *Are all the legs of the stool represented here?* Cross things out, add some things, go wild. Just keep things balanced.

Tuck this little stool picture in your back pocket. Not like your actual physical back pocket but the back of your brain. And whenever you feel like one of your legs is getting wobbly, balance it out again. It's bound to happen, and that's okay. You may even fall over a few times in your life. But if you get back up, well, I'm sure you can see where I'm going with that. The important thing is that you keep on fine-tuning—and remember to take a load off every once in a while. It is a stool, after all.

Now you can put down your pen and finally get into some shit.

chapter

3

Live Like It's Real.

You've got two choices:

1. Put this book on your nightstand and let it collect dust while you tell people that you read it and hope your dreams come true.
2. Do the work.

Most people in your life may never know the difference. This is between you and your god. But can I make a suggestion? Choose the second one.

Having a dream isn't enough to make it come true. I know that, especially with social media, we're used to only seeing the finished product. We see the beach vacations, the clothes, the enormous houses with their ridiculously organized pantries. We don't see the hours sitting at their desk in their mom's apartment, hitting dead ends, sweating it out because the AC window unit is busted, there's only cereal for dinner, and only loose change for paying the bills, then waking up and doing it all over again. We get tricked into thinking we can just fast-forward to the end of the movie. But that ending only has a payoff because of how you got there.

I spent years doing the really hard, really unglamorous stuff. Cleaning toilets. Driving for hours to meetings only to get ghosted. Sending demos to anyone with a US address. Eating shit and grinning like I fucking loved it.

You think that went away once I had my first taste of success? Fuck no. It's one thing to break into the music industry. Then you gotta stay there. The music business is like the Wild West. Nobody needs to have any training and there are no rules.

Then there are the executives looking at the industry money-first, creativity second, and the creatives who are looking at it the other way around. The record labels are gunning for that next hit, and the artists—or at least the good ones—are trying to stay true to themselves. But for every great artist, there's someone who's willing to do anything in order to get their stuff out there. Throw lawyers, managers, and agents into the mix—not to mention ego, status, and money—and it's the Hunger Games, where everyone's running around with spears and knives and swords, but they're the ones who actually like it. Then, just when you think you're good, you hit a trapdoor with a snake pit underneath. That's just the cost of doing business in this industry.

Being great and staying great is a whole other story. Making my own opportunities is *another* whole other story. There's no way I'm coasting right now. There's no way I'm waiting around for people to come to me to make my dreams happen. To be the kind of artist I want to be and create what I want to create, to be an author, a screenwriter, a producer, a founder, I spend *hours* every single day working toward that next big goal. I'm working just as hard at thirty-eight as I was at thirteen. I'm up at 6 a.m. so I have enough time to hang out with my wife and my dogs before I start my calls at 7 a.m. I make time to work out, then it's bouncing between more calls and meetings—about business things, book things, things I'm shooting, events I'm hosting. I'm in the studio, in writing sessions, collaborating with thought partners, collaborating with my manager. And yeah, I talk a big game about taking the time to go for walks and cook myself good food and hang out with my partner and other people who I love—and that's 100 percent true—but that's all just rocket fuel so I can hustle as hard as I can possibly hustle without hitting rock bottom again.

You gotta work hard. I don't mean try hard like one time. You have to live, breathe, eat, shit what you're trying to accomplish. Nobody else is going to do it for you. Nobody is going to call you on the phone one day and say, "Hey, I'm going to make your dreams come true for you." That kind of luck doesn't have your number. *You* have to make it happen. *You* have to want it the most.

And when you want it the most and back it up with the work, do you know what that means? It means that those dreams you have, the ones you listed out for yourself a few pages ago—*they're already real.* I'm not kidding. When I make that list every New Year's Eve with all the things I want to accomplish, I don't start from a place of, "How do I make them real?" I start from a place of "These things are going to happen; it's just a matter of when." Because I'm out there every day working on the *how*. *How* is the hard work. So it's just a matter of time, whether it's days, weeks, or years, that I get to see the payoff.

From the moment you put those goals on paper, they existed. And the way you're going to see the payoff is by living them every day. Starting . . . *right now*.

Make a Plan

You have your list of goals. Great.

You know that you can't bullshit your way out of them. Also great.

And you know that you're going to have to do some work to move toward them. Good.

So now all you need is a plan. A one-step-at-a-time process to get you there.

Yes, it's that simple.

Simple is always better. When I was eighteen or nineteen years old, I was in the studio playing beats for Amanda Ghost, a big-time entertainment executive and songwriter. The beats sounded good, but they were complicated and busy. In technical musical terms: There was a lot of shit going on. Amanda said to me, "These are amazing, but how could someone write a song over this?" She explained that by making the beat a little more sparse or giving it a little more air, someone could really sink their teeth into it. I could always add more stuff later. Now I think of it like a burger. If you've got one that has special sauce and ketchup and caramelized onion and avocado and an egg, first of all, go home and make it yourself because you can do a million times better than the asshole who made it for you. But second of all, it's too much. It's gonna be a mess, and it's not gonna taste good. Now picture a nice, juicy steakhouse patty, maybe some sauce. Maybe an onion. Maybe some pickles. That's what we're going for.

When we first made Justin Bieber's "Love Yourself," it had a full production in it, drums, everything. And then, in the last week before the song had to come out, when it was down to the wire, we stripped it all away and just left the guitar and trumpet. Most people would think that it was too empty and that a pop song needed more accessorizing, but all the other instruments were taking away from the emotion of it. The sparseness made the message that much more powerful.

The same goes for life. Whenever I'm trying to figure out how to do something new, whether it's cooking the best-ever meatballs or writing a book or launching a podcast, I break it down to its most essential parts. I figure out what needs to be there (beef, veal, parmigiano, parsley) and what doesn't (raisins). And I take it one step at a time. Even if one step takes years, I'm still just focusing on that one little step. That's how it looked for the first five years of my career, if not longer. Each year it was one incremental inch toward becoming a true stand-alone producer—produce something with Dr. Luke; make multiple songs as an artist; executive-produce an album; sign and develop artists myself. Each step forward added up to that ultimate goal. One plus one equals two. Or, as my manager says, "The only thing that's rocket science is actual rocket science." Though if I was trying to learn orbital mechanics and propulsion systems, I'd still just take it one step at a time until I cracked it. Probably.

Life is hard enough as it is. Don't overcomplicate things that don't need to be overcomplicated. Changing your life included.

Pick a thing on your list. Ask yourself, "What do I need to do to get from where I am right now to that place?" Then make *that* list. There's no step too small. No idea too dumb. Just look at this chapter: You bought a book about how to achieve success and I told you to go make a plan. Fucking duh.

But it's a crucial step because people are usually so quick to get swept up with this idea of catapulting to greatness that they forget that there's like fifty things they should be doing between here and there. They don't realize that to write their novel, they just need to write ten pages a day. Then they can worry about all the other stuff like giving it a title and finding a literary agent and getting a publishing deal and designing the cover and creating a social media platform for it and planning a book tour.

Some of the items on your list are going to be easy. Let's say you're like me and want to eat more fruit. Do you need to remind yourself to buy it from the grocery store? Do you need to set reminders to go to the kitchen and slice yourself a nectarine? Do you need smoothie recipes so you can stuff a bunch of fruit in a blender and forget about it? Do you need to join a fruit-eating challenge online? Do you need a fruit-eating accountability partner? A daily fruit goal? A weekly fruit goal? You get the idea. I'm going to get some fruit.

Now, some of the things on your list are going to be much bigger and more complicated. But I guarantee you that there's nothing you can't break down into parts. Take, for example, the advice I've given over the years to aspiring artists about how to get noticed in the music industry:

1. Identify a sound that separates you from everyone else.

2. Make that same sound over and over again.
3. Create an identifiable look or a visual language that's associated with your sound. Think about something that differentiates you from everyone else. For me, it's the hair. For Marshmello, it took making music for years to mediocre success, then having his manager suggest wearing the helmet for people to get what he was doing. It doesn't always have to be a schtick, but be the brand.
4. Once you have a song or a collection of songs that you feel confident in, don't wait to get signed—use the internet to release them. Find an interesting way to market them so they'll get noticed. I don't have to tell you that social media was pretty much invented for this. When "Eastside," my first song as an artist, got big, people weren't really connecting it to me. The music video explained who I was as a person, but not who I was as a musician. And I'd made so many songs before that point that people had no idea I'd been a part of—even after they were going viral on TikTok, which had just taken off. So I started making these little videos being like, "I don't know how to do this dance trend but I wrote this song when you were six years old." People started putting two and two together that I'd written all these songs. Then it took on a life of its own with this whole meme

of "benny blanco wrote the Bible"; "benny blanco wrote my textbook." It all started to jell.

5. Build a home base. Find your community that will ride or die just because you're from where they're from or are into what you're into.
6. When it all explodes, add more gasoline to the fire. Be *everywhere*. If I have a new project coming out, you can't escape me. I'm going to be on your podcasts, on your TV, on your feed with three, four posts a day. There's no such thing as too much self-promotion. No one's too cool for that.
7. Put your head down and get back to work.

Every one of these steps applies to pretty much anything you could be thinking about trying. Here, I'll put it in a different context because I'm the kind of dummy who likes things repeated all kinds of ways:

Let's say that I'm an exceptional high school basketball player and I want to go pro. What is the number one thing I need to do? I need to get known. I need my name out there. How am I going to do that from my small town in Ohio?

1. I become my own Times Square billboard. I'm instantly having a few friends record footage of me scoring twenty-five points a game, and I'm making my highlight reel. But it won't just be me

dominating; it's also going to feature my signature move, which for the sake of this scenario we'll say is my windmill dunk.

2. I'm looking up other highlight videos that have gone viral and using that same model. But I'm not just gonna post it online, go to bed, and hope it gets millions of views. I'm going to be sending it to everyone—*SportsCenter*'s Instagram, basketball highlight accounts like Basketball Forever, sports influencers who share all the basketball news. I'm doing everything I can to get it in front of as many eyes as possible.
3. I'm looking up recruiters for the best colleges where I want to play—Duke, UNC, Kentucky—and I'm combing through websites and exhausting every resource to find their phone numbers and email addresses so I can send them that reel.
4. I'm not sitting around waiting to hear back; I'm out there practicing my craft. Getting better and better. If I don't have enough money to hire the best shooting coach in the world, I'm gonna send them my reel or wait for it to go viral and say, "Hey man, I don't have the money to pay you, but I really think that if you invested in me, it will come around tenfold." I'll sell the dream.
5. Then I'm selling everyone else the dream.

In the most basic terms:

1. Figure out your thing and what about you doing that thing is unique.
2. Go out and do it.
3. Let people know about it.
4. Let more people know about it.
5. Keep getting really good at it.

Is this the end of the story? The final word on how you go out there and slay the dragons? Not even close. We're on chapter *three*. Right now we're just talking about what your plan is going to be on paper. You're still at the starting line. You're going to be battling the voices in your head saying you can't do it. You're going to be cycling through endless failures, and you're going to be learning more about yourself and how you show up for other people than you ever thought was necessary for just trying to eat more fruit. But a goal's a goal, and the work is the work. At least now you have a map. And this map is what you can refer to every time you either fall on your face or are ready to advance to the next step.

Start Here

The hardest part of all this is starting. Once you're up and running, you know where you're heading: failure. Well, your goal, too. But before that, most likely failure. Probably more than once. Between each and every step. And every time, you have an opportunity to pause and figure out what you could have done better. Then you get back on the horse and do it again. That's a known quantity now.

Starting, on the other hand, takes some homework. No, homework sucks. We'll call it *investigating*.

The first thing you need to investigate is what about you is unique. In the beginning of my career, I didn't understand how important this was to a plan's success. But realizing that I needed to differentiate myself from everyone else is what ultimately made the biggest impact on my career. The same goes for anyone who's ever left a mark on their industry.

When I was sixteen years old and skipping school to meet with anyone at any record label who said yes, I'd take the Fung Wah bus from DC to New York for ten dollars. For four hours I'd be crammed into a seat that could fit half my ass, there would be no air-conditioning, the windows didn't open, and it smelled like someone pooped and then somehow shoved it up your nostrils. But it was somehow comforting because that meant that I was on my way to getting one step closer to making my dreams come true. Which, in this case, meant interning for a guy named Disco D, a producer who was working with people like 50 Cent, Trick Daddy, and Chamillionaire. I'd been inspired by his avant-garde beats, and he answered one of my many, many Myspace messages where I begged him to let me work for him for free.

I started learning about drum sounds and sound design and vintage synths, which I soaked up while backing up his hard drives and doing pretty much anything else he asked me to just so I could hang around and learn more, which is another story for another chapter because let's just say it was . . . intense.

Meanwhile, I'd been working on my own beats at home. I put together a few of them that I felt like I'd really nailed, then I brought them to my now-manager Andrew, who at the time was answering the phones for the CEO of Atlantic Records, Craig Kallman. He didn't even have his own office, just a cubicle that had a set of computer speakers.

He played the first one and goes, "This one sounds like Timbaland." He presses "next." "This one sounds like Pharrell and the Neptunes." Next. He stops the third track after a second, looks at me, and says, "At Atlantic, we can get beats from Pharrell and Timbaland, so why would we want an imitation from benny from Virginia?"

That messed me up. In the best possible way. I went home, erased every beat I ever made, then spent the next two years trying to make something different that, even if it wasn't very good, at least would let people know it was mine. I needed to create an archetype and a sound that could become a benny blanco sound.

It didn't happen overnight. I cried in my bedroom because I couldn't figure it out, and I'm not really a cry-in-my-bedroom kind of guy. Then, Disco D took his own life at just twenty-six years old. He hadn't just been my mentor and sounding board and one of my greatest teachers who had taught me so much about what is sonically right and wrong—he was one of my best friends. I was crushed. I was too young to understand mental health struggles the way I do now; I had no idea how to process the fact that I didn't have the tools to help him. I wanted to quit. But I heard him in the back of my head telling me what an idiot I'd be if I did. I thought about everything that he'd never get to accomplish. All the things we'd never get to accomplish together. I felt like I had to carry that torch. So I started studying his music and weaving his influence into my own music. I started playing with the mathematical structure that most big pop songs follow, ignoring the rules that an impact has to go into a chorus or that there has to be a hi-hat on the eighth or sixteenth notes to give something movement. But more than anything, I was trying to find a sound that felt fresh and unique. I was done chasing a lesser version of what someone else had done just so I could fit in. I really just wanted to make something that felt cool to *me*.

People thought it was weird. It's hard being the first to do something or do it in a different way than it's been done. It's like growing your hair out—you have to go through that awkward stage where you look kinda dumb with a mullet or bowl cut. You know that once you get past that, you're gonna look like a rock star. But for now, all anyone can tell is that you just have a shitty haircut. And at first, people thought these different types of beats were a very weird, very shitty haircut.

In 2006, while I was interning for Disco D, I met Naeem Juwan, aka Spank Rock. At that time, he was dominating the blog era and making some of the most forward-thinking music I had ever heard. Anytime he came by the studio, I was in awe, even though my only interactions with him were opening the door or bringing him food. I remember walking into the studio to give him his tuna melt when he made direct eye contact and said, "Hey, which verse is better and what rhymes with carrot cake?" In that moment, everything went slow motion and my ears started ringing like a bomb had just exploded at my feet. But once I floated back to reality, I told him my opinions, then froze until he smiled and nodded his head in agreement. From that moment on, it felt like he saw me as a peer and not just another runner in a studio. Over the next few months, he started asking me more questions and bouncing ideas off me. This was huge—I still hadn't found anyone who wanted my beats, and I was looking for any sort of encouragement to grasp onto. It almost felt like I'd made it.

Around that time, I bought a mixtape that mashed up Frank Sinatra with Notorious B.I.G., which also happened to be right around when CeeLo Green and Danger Mouse created Gnarls Barkley. I was on the train listening to that mixtape over and over again when a light bulb went off in my head: *What if I make a collaboration album with a rapper where we sample another artist as the throughline for the whole album?* BINGO! The only problem was that Naeem was the only rapper whose phone number I had. As an idea, it worked—he made a style of music called Baltimore Club, and I wanted to sample a group called 2 Live Crew that brought Miami Bass mainstream. The styles were similar; it was a match made in heaven. But I knew that reaching out to him was a one-shot deal. For days I'd stand in front of the mirror rehearsing what I was going to say to him, until I finally worked up the courage to call. He laughed at me and said no. He thought I was joking.

After Disco D died, Naeem came over to my manager at the time's studio, and we freestyled and got drunk while reminiscing about all the good times we'd had with Disco D. At the end of the night, I finally said to him, my words slurring, "Please get into the studio with me and try this idea . . . *please*." I was basically begging. He chuckled and said something like, "Okay, *finneeee*, benny. You're so annoying." I never thought it would actually come to fruition, but the next week, we went into the studio and recorded a demo. It was the highest high I ever felt. It was like a drug . . . and I'm pretty sure I was much more excited than he was. We didn't speak for weeks after that.

Then one day I got a text from him. He told me that a record label wanted to sign us as a duo. I couldn't believe it. And want to know the craziest part? It was to Downtown Records, *the same people who signed Gnarls Barkley!* If that wasn't fate or karma or some shit, then I don't know what is.

Together, we released the *Bangers & Cash* EP. That then led to Dr. Luke, one of the biggest producers in pop music, taking an interest in me and bringing me on as an apprentice. Which led to me being able to work with people like Britney

Spears, Rihanna, Katy Perry, and Kesha. I became this big "pop" producer, the guy you came to when you wanted a Billboard hit. My songs were at the top of the charts, but I still had aspirations. I wanted to cross genres. I thought I could make great alternative music or rap, but everyone just kept putting me in a box and telling me to stay in my lane. When I stopped listening to them, not only did I have a ton of success in other genres, but I brought back a little piece of those genres to the pop music I was making, which—in my opinion—made it ten times better. Like when we put Wiz Khalifa on Maroon 5's "Payphone" or when we featured Lil Wayne and André 3000 on Kesha's "Sleazy."

It's not easy to do things your own way. It's not. In fact, it's the hardest thing you can do. BUT it's also the one guaranteed way that you're going to end up somewhere more impressive than where you started. And if you at least try, there's a really good bet that eventually, it's gonna be ten times better than if you had done it the way you were told you should, or like everybody else.

The second thing you have to investigate is a little more annoying: *How* are you actually going to get started? Like literally. My first move out of the gate as an aspiring artist wasn't looking for jobs as a producer. No, I started out wanting to get someone to listen to the beats I was making in my tiny room in my mom's tiny condominium. Even if it was on computer speakers in their even shittier cubicle. Because I needed that first yes, which was the key to unlocking a bunch of other yeses.

All the steps I laid out a few pages ago will work. I say smart things sometimes. But you also have to make the process specific to what you want to accomplish. And the way you do that is by researching what exactly that has looked like for other people who have been where you're standing now and have gotten where you want to go. Conveniently, the internet was invented for this.

Then, get involved. Learn everything you need to know directly from the source. Get an internship. Work in the mail room of a talent agency. Work as a runner at a studio. Apprentice yourself to a tailor. See how the sausage is made.

You might have to start back at the bottom. You could have your PhD from MIT, but you're SOL if your dream is to dance professionally. I've put out twenty-nine number one hit songs. I've been nominated for a Grammy twelve times. But when I wanted to act, they weren't like, "Great, here's a show." No, I had to put myself out there and build things from scratch. And because I was working toward something I really wanted, it didn't matter.

Just like it didn't matter when I would take that bus from DC to New York, huffing hot diarrhea air for four hours, to meet a guy who probably couldn't have done anything with my music even if he wanted to. But it was one more person willing to hear about what I was putting out into the world, and he gave me some of the most valuable advice in my entire career. Not to mention the fact that he became my manager and sounding board and partner in attempted world domination.

There's no such thing as a small opportunity. Look at DGC Records. In 1990 they signed Sonic Youth, who weren't by any stretch of the imagination a mainstream group at the time. But DGC would have never gotten Nirvana to leave Sub Pop if they didn't have Sonic Youth.

Even after I'd become a successful producer, I wanted to make an album with an independent artist called Francis and the Lights. I basically had to do it for free; it took me about two years to put together; and it wasn't commercially successful at all. Everyone told me I was crazy. But I believed in the project because I believed in him as an artist. I believed in making the best music I could, which is what inspired me and continues to inspire me. Not whether something is going to be big or make a lot of money. And by doing that, all these huge artists who I wasn't working with now wanted to work with me. I got a call from Kanye West because he heard that album and said it moved him. A week later, it was the Weeknd. By not choosing the money and following my heart, I got my cake *and* took a big, delicious bite.

My wife, Selena, and I talk about this all the time and about how the "smaller" opportunities over the course of our careers have been some of the most meaningful. She's constantly being asked to be the lead in romantic comedies that will probably go on to make hundreds of millions of dollars but she'd rather do an avant-garde French musical about a trans drug dealer. Not because she had any idea it would go on to set a world record for the most-nominated non-English-language film in Academy Award history. She'd much rather take a risk on a show or movie that's going to impact culture than be the star of something mediocre that'll be forgotten tomorrow. Add that to the list of many reasons why I love her.

Bottom line: Pick an idea or goal, make a plan, figure out how to do it your way, then figure out where to start, no matter how small it might feel. I didn't say any of this wouldn't sound dumb. But it works.

And luckily, you won't be doing it alone.

Find a Mentor

If you were growing up in Reston, Virginia, in the 1990s, there weren't expectations that you'd achieve great things. Graduating high school and getting married was the big time. There wasn't anyone to look up to. So when I decided in elementary school that I was going to be the biggest artist of all time, I realized that I was going to have to find someone who could teach me how. I wanted a front-row seat to watch someone doing the work, ideally someone who would let me get my hands dirty, too.

My first mentor was a guy in my brother's fraternity, Sam Trockey. He had a recording studio, knew how to make music, and had had a few small successes. When I was thirteen, Sam was the first person to put me in the studio and teach me how to use Pro Tools. He then introduced me to a guy named

Jonathan Shecter, who was the founding editor in chief of *The Source*, put out some of Eminem's early records, and had a lot of ties to people in the hip-hop community like 50 Cent and Nas. He taught me the ins and outs of the music business. How you get signed to a record deal, how a budget works. The boring stuff that young artists rarely learn early in their career and make huge mistakes because of it. He also taught me how to carry myself in meetings, to chill out when I'd get overexcited. I learned that there's a thin line between being annoying and persistent. After that came my Myspace campaign for Disco D to take me on as an intern, followed by Dr. Luke and Max Martin.

They were the ones who taught me the art of songwriting—more specifically, how to make the perfect pop song. There was a mathematical precision to their work, like making sure there's not a ton of bass leading up to the chorus, adding an abrupt stop, then adding a ton of bass in along with impact sounds like sixteenth notes to add urgency. They taught me dynamics, or making sure that a song is like a roller coaster in the best possible way. It's not all speed and crazy drops—that doesn't feel good. But when there's a slow rise, then a drop, then some turns, maybe another slow-down, maybe another drop, then it feels like a full experience. But more than anything, they taught me to never settle. Most people stop working on a song when it's 75 percent of the way done. Seventy-five is good. It's passable. It might even get radio play. But that extra

25 percent is what makes a song stand the test of time. It's not settling for lyrics that are just pretty good. It's trying the chorus over multiple different productions. It's banging your head against the wall until every inch of that song is right. To this day I've never done it any other way.

Every one of these individuals shaped who I became as an artist. Whether they knew it or not, every one of them is the reason why I went on to accomplish what I did. Because as much as I could look up YouTube videos about writing beats or producing albums or read some kind of book or take some kind of class, there's nothing that compares to real-life experience to show you what to do. And also what *not* to do morally and craftsmanship-wise, which is equally part of the learning experience. All of that wisdom is part of the mentor lineage. And that's how you get better.

So go out and find that person for you. Tell them you'll do anything for them—be their assistant, clean their toilets, shine their shoes. Whatever it takes for you to just sit there and watch them do what they do. It's going to give you everything you need to know, or at the very least, a running start.

Find a Collaborator

When I sit down with an artist, a lot of the time it's because there's a song, an album, an idea, a feeling, *something* that they've been carrying around but can't figure out how to get down on the page. So they come to me. That's not because they're bad at their job. These are some of the best performers and songwriters and musicians in the world. It's because when you're *so close* to an idea, when it is in your soul, your bones, your DNA, you start to get tunnel vision. You lose perspective. You have no idea if the direction you're walking in is leading you toward something really, really great, or the shittiest song you've ever made.

Sometimes I sit down with them and it takes a few hours to untangle all the junk they've been hoarding in their brains about this idea. We take it out, take a step back, look at it all, and figure it out. Other times, just having me in the room—not even saying a damn thing—is enough for them to take a breath and let it start to flow.

As much as I'd like to think that's all because I'm really good at what I do, I know a big part of what makes me so successful is that . . . I'm not them. I'm just another person in the room, giving them the perspective they need, and letting them know that they're doing a good job. *Everyone* needs that. No matter where they are in their career.

Ed Sheeran, who has an absolute shitload of number one hits, more awards than I could be bothered to count, and can sell out an international stadium tour, came to my house a few years ago to play me his new album. He hadn't put out music in a while and he was petrified that he might never have a big song again. He played me "Bad Habits," which he was particularly worried wasn't going to work. Fast-forward a few months, and that song is a massive hit. I didn't necessarily have to do anything—not in a professional sense—but being there as a sounding board and telling him that he's got this was as valuable as anything else I could have done for him in that moment.

The opposite is also true. Sometimes you need someone to tell you how bad your idea is. When I first started toying around with becoming an artist after spending years writing and producing songs for other people, I had this avant-garde vision. I wanted to create an alter ego for myself, just completely reinvent who I was in order to reintroduce myself to the world in this new capacity. I had this mask that I was going to wear at all times so it would be super mysterious who I was, and I was playing around with this kind of weird, artistic, highbrow new sound to go with it. I didn't really know what kind of music I wanted to make as part of this whole experiment, but I was fixated on this idea. I was all in.

One day I was talking with Cashmere Cat, a DJ and producer I collaborate with sometimes. I showed him the mask, told him all about my vision, and then asked him, "Hey, what type of music do you think I should make?" Because I was really stuck trying to figure it out.

He had no idea what I was talking about. He was just like, "Make the music you always make. Why are you not just being yourself?" And it blew my mind that *I'd never even thought of that*. It hadn't once crossed my mind that the solution could be as simple as "be you." There's just nothing as valuable as someone being like, "Dude, X is there and Y is there and Z is there—just put it together and you're good."

I love collaborating because it's hard to be all alone and know whether the ideas are good or bad. I love having a sounding board. I love being able to put a mediocre idea out there, then build and build and build. Or having someone say something completely random that sparks an even better idea. I love the energy of someone being there, hyping me up. If I finish a song or a demo and nobody's around, the first thing I do is call everyone I know to play it for them because I want to feel that hype. Even if it's my mom telling me she can't wait to hear what I've been working on, then literally the moment I press play asking me what I want for dinner. It's just my blood, sweat, and tears, Mom. No big deal. But it still feels good.

Find a collaborator. Even if they're completely "unqualified," whatever that means, find someone who is willing to be around for the hard stuff. Who will sit in the room smelling your own farts with you until you can crack whatever it is that you set out to work on. Someone you can call when you're stuck. When you need to test something out. When you're not sure about something. Someone who isn't afraid to tell you that you're an idiot. Or that you're a genius.

Because once you know that you're a little bit more of the latter and a little bit less of the former, you're gonna have a much easier time taking the big swings and moving on to that next crucial step.

Fake the Funk

Here's a fun fact: You're never going to feel ready to start. If you wait around until you feel prepared or like you have enough experience or like you know how it all works, I will come back to check on you in five years and you will still be standing exactly where you are right now.

Nobody actually knows how to do anything. We're all just guessing. Nobody knows how to become a professional athlete. Nobody knows how to start a company. Most of the time we're learning on the job after we've already gotten that job. You might be able to call yourself a doctor after graduating from medical school, but you need to learn how to actually be a doctor for like seven more years beyond that. If those people can be out there full-on saving people's lives before they're even licensed to practice medicine, then what is your excuse?

Success is not worrying about the inevitable failure that comes from not totally knowing what you're doing. It's about going all in with so much conviction that everyone believes you—including yourself—then rolling the dice. It's a slightly smarter version of "fake it till you make it." Or a nicer way of telling you to, yet again, shut up and go. Because when you're out there talking about whatever it is you want to do like it's real, putting it into practice like it's real, and showing up every day like it's real, it becomes real—even if there are hard lessons along the way.

It's 2007. I'm nineteen years old. I had no records and a virtually nonexistent résumé, but my manager Andrew is A&R-ing a baby band by the name of 3OH!3. For those of you who don't know what an A&R rep is, think of them as someone who holds a musician's hand through the process of making an album. Typically they sign the artist, find them producers and songwriters to work with, figure out the budgets, deal with the label on their behalf, etc. Okay, back to the story. This group essentially had no budget, so I was an easy yes for them because I was dirt cheap and willing to buy my own ticket from New York to a small town in Maryland and schlep my own keyboard because they couldn't afford rentals. I'd also never really front-line run making a record before, a detail we'd conveniently left out.

I arrive at the house we're recording at. It was owned by a producer named Matt Squire, who was responsible for basically every pop punk album coming out at the time. Everyone from Panic! At the Disco to Plain White T's. I wasn't nervous at all. I remember just blurting out, "All right guys, take me to the studio," as soon as I walked in the door. We went into a creepy basement, and at the end of this dark hallway was this state-of-the-art studio that felt like either a dream or the start of a horror movie, but either way, I was all in. We hit it off and started working on their preexisting demo. It was a cool song, but deep down I thought we could do something better.

Early into our session, Matt said, "I gotta go out of town for the weekend; have fun!" So later that night, after I'd finished up what I'd come out to do, I started hearing that voice inside me saying I needed to try to make a song from scratch with these guys. I knew they didn't have a song that could be considered their lead single yet (even though in their mind the album was done and ready to mix). I also knew that I'd never made a song from scratch with a signed artist in the room. But I wasn't going to let that stop me.

So we're getting drunk, making vlogs, and I just casually said, "Hey . . . guys . . . let's . . . start a new idea." I walked over to the Juno-106 keyboard and started moving the knobs, creating a sound; then Nat Motte walked over and started playing some notes. Now, I know this is going to sound cliché, but the next two and a half hours were almost a blur, and by the time I came out of the fever dream, we had a song. A real, finished song. The entire time I had been acting like I knew exactly what I was doing, completely bullshitting my way through the session—I had never even recorded a live guitar before. I knew absolutely nothing except the fact that I had a hunger and wouldn't give up until I willed my future into existence.

The guys ended up loving the song and performed it on the Warped Tour all summer long. More than a year later, it went number one on radio. What's even crazier is that in that one-year span, I made *Circus* with Britney Spears plus "I Kissed a Girl" and "Hot N Cold" with Katy Perry. And for some reason, they all popped at the same time.

If I hadn't gone into that basement in Maryland with such blind confidence and attempted to nail a first single for a band who thought their album was already done besides a few production tweaks, then I never would have had that moment.

So I just kept doing that. The first time I put out a song as an artist and had to write an album rollout plan. The time I auditioned for *Dave*. When I decided to write a cookbook. When I became an executive marketing consultant for Epic Games. I didn't know how to do any of those things. But I gave them my best shot and made them a reality.

My friend Matty Matheson is another great example of this. For years people knew him as a successful chef, restaurateur, and *New York Times* bestselling cookbook author. A food guy. Then Christopher Storer asked him to be the culinary consultant for the pilot episode of *The Bear*. And then Chris asked him if he could act. Matty could have been honest and admitted he had no idea. Or he could go with what he ultimately said, which was, "Yeah, I guess so." They put him on, the show got picked up and won pretty much every award possible, and it opened a whole new world in TV and film for Matty. All because he lived like it's real.

Remember, it *is* already real. Your job is to live like that's true. I'm not a big woo-woo *The Secret* positive affirmation person, but when I want something to happen, I'm putting that out in the Universe/to my friends/to my team/to the cashier at Gelson's every day. If I want to do another album and I want it to come out next year, I tell everyone with a straight face that I'm working on an album and that it's coming out next year—even though I have no idea what it is and haven't done a single thing to make it happen. But once I say it, it's gospel. What, am I going to be a liar and go back on my word? Am I going to backtrack to "maybe"? No, I'm going to work my ass off until it comes true. Or I get to that first step of making it come true, and then the second. Mostly because I don't want to look like an idiot. Also because I'm now living in the version of reality where I have an album that's coming out next year.

When it comes to faking the funk, you gotta be your own best advertiser. Every new thing I do, I'm campaigning on it like I'm running for president because if I believe it, they believe it. If they believe it, everyone believes it. My cookbook is a great example of this. I've always loved cooking, and there has always been this little voice in the back of my head that made me think I might want to be a chef. The music just happened to take off first.

But that didn't turn off that little voice. So in my early twenties I'd throw dinner parties to scratch the itch and tell the world, *Yeah, this is who I am too*. At first maybe five people would come. Then twenty. Then fifty. Then a hundred. They became these kinda cool, if-you-know-you-know type things. One day, my friend Jake Cohen was telling his literary agent, Sarah Passick, about these parties. He suggested reaching out to see if I wanted to write a book, and she did. We threw around a bunch of ideas of what that book could be, and the one that scared me the most was a cookbook. I wasn't a classically trained chef. I had no idea what I was doing in the kitchen. And I definitely had no idea how to write a book. But I did what I do best when something scares the shit out of me. I said, "Let's do it."

It would have been the easiest thing in the world to say, "No, thank you." Sarah would go find her next client, and I'd go make my next album. I wouldn't have to spend months of my life figuring out how many cups are in a serving of curried chicken salad and worrying about whether people would even want to listen to what I had to say just because I was some idiot who sometimes makes good music. I could just go to sleep and rest easy knowing that the next morning I'd wake up, and my life would go on exactly as it had been—which was pretty great.

But I said yes. Because it was another mess that I got to make. Another opportunity to fumble my way through something, pretending that I knew what I was doing but really soaking up all this new information on a new topic that made me really excited. And I knew that was the bigger win for me personally. For that little voice. So I spent the next two years turning my dream into a reality. I went out looking for any insight I could get from everyone from Michelin-starred chefs to home cooks on Instagram. I went to fancy restaurant kitchens in New York City to learn from Japanese omakase masters and to the apartments of twentysomethings who knew how to make the perfect French dip. I was a sponge. I knew how to cook already, but it didn't matter because there's always something new to learn. I teamed up with Jess Damuck, a friend and cookbook author who helped me figure out how to actually put all my ideas together. For a little while, things went badly—because everything *I* did was wrong. I had no idea how different cooking at home was from creating a recipe for a book, how precise and specific everything had to be. I had to remake recipes millions of times. Then I got the idea to ask friends to contribute some of their favorite recipes or to make my recipes better. And slowly, over time, things started to go my way.

Then I needed to convince the world that I was a good enough cook to write a cookbook. So about a year out from the launch, I started telling people who weren't just my friends how much I loved to cook. I focused on putting up food content, collaborating with experts like Matty Matheson and Tieghan Gerard, going to food events, speaking at food events.

I was also honest with people. I said, *Hey, I might not be a Michelin-trained chef, but I am a guy who likes to make food for people I care about, and if I could do that and write it down in a cookbook, then it'll be really easy for you too.* And that struck a chord. People loved the idea of this average dude making above-average food.

Then, about a week after the book was released, I was in a used-furniture store somewhere in Texas when my agent called me. She was crying. Then she proceeded to tell me that we'd made the *New York Times* bestseller list. And that little voice in the back of my head said, *You did it.* If I hadn't taken that chance or told that little white lie—"Of course I can make a cookbook"—then stepped up to the plate full of full-blown bullshit, I wouldn't be where I am today. That goes for almost everything else in my life. This all exists because of sheer will and innocent deception.

We're all just bullshitting. Eventually we accumulate all these hours of experience, and the bullshit slowly fades. But then we beat the level and start a new one, and it immediately begins all over again.

You will never know until you jump into the deep end whether you can swim (metaphorically). My bet is that you won't be able to float—because I'm pretty sure only toddlers can do that—so you're gonna *have* to swim. And maybe, just maybe, you'll get a couple laps in. And then a couple more.

So fuck it; cannonball in. I'll save you a towel.

Get Lost

From the time I was ten years old, I thought I was going to be the biggest rapper in the world. I truly believed that. I told anyone who came within fifty feet of me that it was just a matter of time. My friends didn't believe me. My parents didn't believe me. I think I might have been the only person in the world who believed me. So I did everything I could to make it happen.

I annoyed people until they wouldn't answer my phone calls anymore. I slept on train station floors. I begged friends for money to pay for train tickets, promising I'd pay them back when I hit it big. When I wasn't making my mom drive me to freestyle competitions where the grand prize was five hundred dollars, she was taking me out to recording studios in Atlantic City and Philadelphia—to anyone who would have me. I would blindly do anything for anyone who said they had connections in the music business, which didn't amount to anything other than my mom's house getting robbed. Twice.

I didn't become the world's biggest rapper. But I did make it. Because all that time I was paying my dues. I was learning. So when I pivoted to becoming a songwriter and producer, I wasn't starting from scratch. Then, after twenty years of that career, I came back to my artistry and made music with my own name on it. And cooked food and wrote about it. And was on a TV show. And wrote scripts and scores and all kinds of things I never really set out to do. Which is a long-winded way of saying just keep rocking. Because there's no such thing as wrong experience, and it's pointless to get hung up on where you're going to end up.

I've been able to do some pretty cool stuff in music *because* I was willing to be flexible and follow the dream as it unfolded. Because I never saw my career as a single path that had to look a certain way. There were a few places I wanted to get to, but I never had a map. The only choice I had was to walk out my front door and trust that the choices I made along the way would get me there. Getting lost *was* the path.

Look at the guys who started YouTube—they couldn't find a video of Janet Jackson's breast falling out during the Super

Bowl, so they made a video-sharing site. Viagra started as a heart medication until they realized a side effect was your dick exploding through your pants. I don't think a single person here would be mad if their wrong left turn ended up being one of the highest-grossing companies of all time.

This chapter is about you going out there and working your ass off. I know that right now you're worried about where it's all gonna land. So much worrying. Seriously, don't you have anything better to do? I say this with so much love: There's no point to worrying because you're definitely *not* gonna land exactly where you thought you would. It might be similar. It might be close. But I'll bet money that it won't be exact. And that's cool. Better than cool—it's *lucky*. If you're putting the work in, if you're paying attention, if you're not sedentary and crying about your life and what you think you can't do, you're good. You're gonna end up *somewhere*. There are going to be pivots and changes of plans. There are going to be new things that catch your attention because you didn't even know those opportunities existed. Or you hadn't considered them before.

Sometimes the primary goal you have needs a quick pause. For me, there are times when the music doesn't come. There's nothing necessarily wrong, I'm just not connecting creatively the way I want to. And you can't force it. You can't muscle through something like that. That's when I go to other outlets like writing television shows and cookbooks. To you it looks like I'm out there climbing other mountains, and yeah, I kinda am, but it's also because I'm still at base camp for this other thing that I'm "supposed" to be great at. Which is a lot of pressure for a person. So I take a step off the path and start a new one. But they all lead me to the same place—feeling creatively satisfied.

Looking back at the last fifteen, twenty years of my career, I can see all the places where my path got a little bit squiggly. There were side quests and tangents, but they all got me to where I am now. I reserve the right to make a million squiggles and doodles. Frankly, if your life's aerial view doesn't look like a Keith Haring painting, you're doing it wrong.

See where things take you. Maybe nowhere, but also, maybe beyond what you originally imagined.

Leave It All on the Field

It was 2010 and we were done with Kesha's debut album, *Animal.* Done, done. It already had a release date, which meant we had to turn it over to the label, like, yesterday. But at the last minute, just before I hit send, I felt like it needed something else. I couldn't tell you what; it's just something I do—try to put more songs on, try to exhaust every possible option, until the label starts making threats on my life. Nothing's finished until it's finished. So we made three more songs. They were "TiK ToK," "Your Love Is My Drug," and "Take It Off"—what became three of the four singles on the album and three of her biggest songs.

Even now, when I could probably do what I do in my sleep, I'm still always trying to beat myself. I've always had that mindset of just when you think you're done, you push a little harder. Most of the people I know who are really good at what they do are the same way. In 2014, Ed Sheeran came over to play me his new album. It was due to be turned in, but he'd added a few new bonus songs last-minute, and he wanted to know if they should be on the album. One of them was "Thinking Out Loud." I told him it was the biggest hit I have ever heard, and then we slow-danced like we were married and laughed.

SZA is also the definition of someone who isn't done until she's done. The week she was the musical guest on *Saturday Night Live* in 2022 was the same week her album *SOS* was coming out. She'd stay up all night after rehearsals, changing songs up until the very last second because she knew she could beat them and make better ones.

My friend Dave Burd, who you might know as Lil Dicky, has what he calls the "No Stone Unturned Method." He exhausts every detail of everything he does to the point where everyone hates him during the process. About five years ago, he came up with the song title "Good Guy," and he wanted to do something where it was him and another rapper over this sinister mafioso-type beat basically battling over what good guys they are, like opening the door for people or remembering when a friend doesn't like pickles on their burger. I had probably done forty to sixty versions of that song, and he still didn't think it was good enough. And yeah, I kinda hated him in the moment, but then the song came out and it was amazing. I have total respect for his process. "Freaky Friday," "Earth"—all his songs take three to four years to make. He hasn't put out an album in ten years. Because he doesn't want to look back on it and think, "I could have done more." He refuses to leave anything to "what if?" Because of that, he has the ability to make a song ten times better. Or a script ten times better.

I'm a perfectionist, so I feel that regret on some level all the time. I'm always listening to songs of mine that have already come out and thinking, *Ugh, why's that hi-hat so loud?* or *Ugh, I wish I changed that harmony*. And they're like number one hits. But if I'm being honest with myself, I know that in the moment of making that song, I most likely agonized over that hi-hat or that harmony. And that it ended up where it did because, at the time, it was the best that it could possibly be. When I'm supposed to be finished with a song, they have to pry it out of my hands. I'm never not trying to do better.

Like Dave, I don't want to look back and think I didn't do everything possible to ensure something could be great. If something doesn't work out after all that, because sometimes it just doesn't, then that's okay. You can live with that. But if it doesn't work out and you have to admit to yourself that there was something else you could have done, then that's going to be the itch you can't scratch in the middle of your back.

Now that you're going out there to chase these big, fat dreams of yours, you have to leave it all on the field. You have to fully commit. Yes, there will be moments when it won't work out. Obviously. We know that. And we'll talk more about what to do when that most definitely happens. But I never, ever want it to be because you weren't willing to let it rip. There is no plan B.

My mom was always asking me what my backup plan was going to be. When I told her I wasn't going to college because I wanted to learn from the real world and not some textbook or dead guy, when I told her that I wanted to make music instead of getting a "real job," even after I told her that I was going to Los Angeles to work with Britney Spears at twenty years old, she'd say, "What's your plan B?" There's never been a plan B. And there shouldn't be. Unless the condom ripped, then it's a miracle of modern medicine. But if you want something in life? You have to go get that thing. You can't settle for the second-best thing. And the way you get that thing and keep that thing and keep climbing for the next thing is to:

Work. Fucking. Hard.

c[redacted]er

4

Fail Until It Feels Good.

Success happens when you meet failure in a dark alley, alone, at night. Are you gonna let it kick your ass, then lie there crying and moaning for the rest of your life? Are you gonna go home and whine about how you would have won the fight if only it hadn't been arms day at the gym? Or are you gonna take that beating, wipe the blood and snot from your face, then ask for a second helping?

It's the last one. That's the right answer. Because even though you might get your teeth knocked out, there's a good chance that you'll get a couple more licks in than you did the round before. Eventually, you'll get stronger. Your moves will get better. Every bad guy you take down is preparing you for the final boss until you could run attack combos in your sleep. You might get a little busted up, but that's the good pain.

There are countless moments when I could have curled up into a ball, sucked my thumb, and cried uncle.

I could have quit believing I could be anything I wanted to be when my parents told me my dreams were a waste of time.

I could have quit trying to become a musician when I was thirteen years old and writing hundreds of messages on Myspace to labels and managers and writers, then getting told no or winding up ghosted by almost every one of them.

I could have quit when I was on my knees scrubbing toilets for Disco D because I told him I'd do *anything* to work for him and he agreed to let me come up from Virginia to New York City on the weekends. I could have quit when I had to install a television in one of his offices for a meeting and he took this huge bamboo stick and started hitting me on the back for not doing it quickly enough. I could have quit when he poured milk and cereal on my head in front of everyone because I'd apparently bought the wrong groceries for him. I could have quit when he'd send me to seven different places around Manhattan and Brooklyn where the train service was really unreliable and it'd be raining and he'd scream at me for being late. Or when he'd yell at me to "get the fuck out of the room and go home" if I tried speaking in meetings. And I definitely could have quit when I finally got the opportunity to play my beats for him, and he took my entire hard drive, threw it out of the window, and said, "Start again."

I didn't quit, because I wanted more for my life than sticking around Reston, Virginia, getting married at twenty-one, having kids, never leaving, and never giving myself a chance to do what I knew I was born to do.

I didn't quit, because I was unwilling to accept defeat.

I didn't quit, because even though I was in a legitimately toxic, abusive relationship with Disco D, in his own messed-up way, he was pushing me forward. I honestly believe he was the hardest on me out of all the interns because he knew I'd be the most successful based on my work ethic and skill set. I also knew that he would never want me to quit. So I never did.

I ended up meeting Spank Rock while he was recording in Disco D's studio. He was the first person to believe in my beats. Which led to me getting signed to a record label. Which led to me getting my first record deal.

You don't stop needing a barf bag for the ups and downs after you "make it," either. In 2013, I had my first "cold streak." As far as anyone could tell, I was crushing. Because of the delay that happens between when you finish working on something and when it gets released, songs that I'd made a year or two prior were coming out and blowing up—OneRepublic's "If I Lose Myself," Iggy Azalea's "Black Widow," Maroon 5's "Animals," Ed Sheeran's "Don't." I'd won the Songwriters Hall of Fame Hal David Starlight Award, which is given to "gifted songwriters who are at an apex in their careers and are making a significant impact in the music industry via their original songs." Their words. Also, thank you. Everyone was constantly telling me, "Man, you're killin' it!"

But none of that was based on any of the new stuff I was creating. At that exact "apex moment," I was bottoming out. A song of mine didn't work. Then another one. They had no cultural impact, no chart position. They weren't seen as anything special, just big ol' steamin' turds. Then nobody wanted any of my new songs. I wasn't the shiny new toy anymore. The labels wanted the hot new producer making fresh records, so the people who would normally take risks on me were looking elsewhere.

This went on for *two* years.

I had been riding on such a high and then the rug was pulled out from under me. All these things I thought were a lock weren't. It was the first time in a long time that I'd experienced adversity on that level. I was walking down the street in New York talking to Andrew, my manager, on the phone, on the verge of tears, letting him know that this is the end. This is when I pack it all up and move on to something else. It had been a good run. *Too* good a run, actually. I was so angry with myself for not enjoying the good stuff while it lasted. I was almost pleading with him, asking him, "What are we doing wrong?"

He said: "Stay the course. Keep doing what you're doing. It's going to come back around."

For some reason, I believed him.

It made me realize that I was tired of people saying who could be on a song, how many songs could be on the album, which songs went to radio, how many videos I could make, what they would be like, what the promotion would be like—all these things you deal with as a songwriter-producer. I wanted to sign my own artists. Put out my own things. So I wrapped up my weeklong mope and started a record label, Mad Love Records, as an imprint of Interscope Records. I signed artists like Cashmere Cat, Jessie Ware, and Tory Lanez.

The year 2015 ended up being one of the biggest I had professionally. Justin Bieber's "Love Yourself" hit number one. Vance Joy's "Fire and the Flood" hit number one. Selena's "Same Old Love" hit number one. In 2016, three more number ones. Then in 2017, I got Grammy nominations for Best R&B Song, Song of the Year, Album of the Year, and Producer of the Year.

All because I didn't curl up into that ball and quit.

All because I recognized the *opportunity* that "failing" gave me—pressing pause and pivoting.

All because I had amnesia about failure.

All because I had patience. I learned that sometimes the

moment is just not right now. But it definitely could be later. And that when it looks like people are having overnight success, it's been a decade in the making.

All because I learned how to trust my gut.

All because I knew how to keep myself amped.

Failure is part of the process. Eventually it'll start to feel good. It's only the end of the process if you let it be.

Have Amnesia

It was 2009 (or maybe it was 2010). I was supposed to go to Los Angeles to work on Katy Perry's album *Teenage Dream*. I had just stopped flying, so I bribed my brother, Jeremy, to drive me across the country in his RAV4 in exchange for a Hugo Boss suit. It took us more than a week to get to LA. I finally get out of the car, get to take off my shoes and lie down when my phone rings—Dr. Luke and Max Martin, the godfathers of pop music, tell me to come to the studio.

I'm exhausted but I go. And as soon as I walk through the door, the first thing Luke says is, "We did it; we finished the album. It's done!" Then they immediately play "Part of Me" and "The One That Got Away" while jumping up and down and cheering at each other. To recap: I just drove all the way from New York for zero reason. As in, this really great opportunity that got me to even *consider* spending a week driving to LA had passed me by. I'd failed. I was a loser.

With my head down and my tail between my legs like a

football player who just lost the big game, I wander to the lounge because what else was I supposed to do? Tell them they should have waited seven days so I could travel by horse like it's the 1400s? Invent time travel? No, I do the only thing I know how to do: Get over it. I take out this twenty-dollar mini keyboard I'd gotten at a garage sale and a guitar, and I start making beats. Maybe it was because the thought of getting back into the car was enough to make me want to murder somebody. Maybe it was my coping mechanism to think, *What if I just go and make something better?* All I know is that most people would have waved their flag.

But there I was with this silly little setup. Luke comes in and lays down some guitars and basses. Then Max walks in to get a cookie. He hears the beats and starts humming something under his breath. Before I know it, we'd come up with two rough demos. Over the next two weeks, me, Max, Luke, Katy, and Bonnie McKee worked on those little ideas made in the kitchen of this huge recording studio, which would become "Teenage Dream" and "California Gurls" and would change Katy's career forever. Honestly, the only reason it took so long is because we had to rewrite "Teenage Dream" seven times just to get the lyrics right.

The moral of this story is not that I manage to pull successes out of my ass.

The moral is that you gotta have amnesia about failure.

If you're gonna move past the disasters, setbacks, no's, and fuck-you's, you gotta shake 'em off. All the greats do. They lose.

They mess up. They miss. All the time. We remember them as winners *because* they didn't accept those outcomes as the final word. Michael Jordan shot the ball more than any other player in the NBA, but no one was sitting there saying, "Did you see how many three-pointers he missed today?" No, everyone was just mesmerized by him hitting the game-winner while fading away with his tongue out. Roger Federer, who won 80 percent of his 1,526 singles matches, only won *54 percent* of the individual points.

Winners aren't winning all the time; they're just winning slightly more than they're losing. And they're definitely not hanging on to the other 46 percent. I'm not a sports psychologist, but I'm pretty sure that if athletes are anything like the people I know who have gotten to the top of their field, then they're looking at those losses as opportunities to figure out where they went wrong, how to improve, and how to do better next time. And I'll tell you what they're *not* doing—they're definitely not wallowing. It's okay to feel your feelings when you get knocked down. It's okay to mope. But then it's time to move on. We got shit to do, guys. What would you rather do, be sad forever? Beat yourself up forever? Okay, fine, keep wallowing, but at least do it while you start working on the next attempt. For real, though—what else is there to do but keep moving forward?

For me, 95 percent of the music I make during the year or scores I write or ideas I have for TV shows don't ever make it out into the world. About 5 percent make it to the finish line—and of those, like one, maybe two things are big successes. How's that for numbers? Does that make me a failure? What failure? New number.

About seven years ago, I was working on my second album as an artist, *Friends Keep Secrets 2*. I had gotten a *massive* artist to agree to do a song with me, like one of the biggest artists in the world. We wrote a song, recorded it, mastered it, even, made a video treatment. The week before we were supposed to shoot the music video, they pulled out.

This is extremely out of the ordinary. It's common for songs to not come to fruition, but never this far into the process. I'd been working on this album for *three years*. I'd released some songs (that weren't successful) along the way, had gone back to the drawing board a few times, and now I finally had an album I was proud of. We'd set up an extensive marketing rollout, and this song was the glue that held the entire project together. And this person just walked away.

I tried going back to them. I tried fixing the situation. I even tried begging. I texted their manager. Crickets. Radio silence. They never answered me again. My confidence had been shattered. I was thinking

There's no way I could go through all of this again.

I can't go back to the drawing board another time.

It's over.

Wait, it's over? Am I finished? Should I quit music?

For an entire day, I was a puddle, trying to figure out what I would do for a living now that I'd quit being a producer and realized I suck at everything and have no other talent or skills.

Then I figured I might as well try again. What other option was there? Roll over and die? Of course I doubted myself. I definitely questioned my life choices. But I didn't let it define me. I dug deep for whatever shred of gratitude I could find for that experience; then I put my energy into moving on to the next thing. Instead of expending it all on wishing for what could have happened, I got back to work making the album.

About six months later, I'm in the studio with Finneas. I'd known him for years, and we'd been in the studio together a bunch of times. But it wasn't always us making music. Sometimes we'd get in there and just talk for, like, four hours. Because I'm never gonna press it. I'm never gonna pressure someone to crank something out. It's never, "Oh, we gotta make a hit today." When you force it is when you make dog shit. It's too much pressure. I'd much rather eat some good food and get in some good chat. When everyone is comfortable and stops overthinking, that's when the magic happens.

Back to that evening with Finneas in the studio. We are making this fast, more straightforward pop song, and I had this feeling in my stomach that it wasn't right. We finish, he's packing up all his stuff, and I just blurt out, "Ughhh, Finneas, I want one of those ballads you're so good at for my album—anyone can make an up-tempo song that could be on the radio, but I want one of those beautiful songs you make that no one else can. . . . I wanna cry." He sat back down at the Wurlitzer. It was during the Covid lockdown, so we'd been talking about how people were going through it and how isolating it could be. And we got on the topic of how artists at the top can feel alone or empty inside, like they don't have anyone to talk about their feelings with. We started writing from Justin Bieber's perspective, and thirty minutes later, we had written a demo that would eventually become "Lonely."

Justin was in Canada, and not being able to be in the studio together made it difficult to get the song across the finish line, so it took about six months until we finally had a finished product we felt good about.

That single did end up being a huge hit from my album. But show me the moment in that story where the success of that song or that album was obvious. You can't. Because it wasn't. To anybody, least of all me. But I chose to go along for the ride instead of finding reasons to give up. Maybe that's where it should have been the most obvious.

The real icing on the cake, though, was when I ended up reaching out to the original artist and telling them that I wished them the best—because I'm a nice guy and always want to be doing the right thing. I said, "I was really bummed out in the moment, but I wanted to thank you because I wouldn't have dug down deep enough to find that next song and have it mean so much to me in this moment now." Then we hugged and went on to be best friends.

Just kidding, they were a huge dick about it.

And *then,* when that artist eventually came back to me years later to see if I wanted to work together, I passed and told them that I didn't feel great about how things had gone down. Because boundaries. But you don't have to worry about that until chapter 6.

People are going to screw things up for you and you're going to have to keep going as though nothing happened. Sometimes *you're* going to screw things up for you and you're going to have to keep going.

The day before Yom Kippur, I was working on "We R Who We R" for Kesha's deluxe version of *Animal + Cannibal.* The last 15 to 20 percent of producing a song is always the most arduous process, so I needed something to make finishing it more exciting. So I decided to take an edible. Bad idea. Just as the THC was coursing through my veins, I had to restart the computer because it froze; it felt like it took three to four hours to come back up when it was probably closer to fifteen seconds. Everything was moving in slow motion. I was sweating, making strange noises. The assistant engineer looked at me and said, "Yooooooooo, youuuuuuu doooooon't loooook sooooo goooood." I called my brother and begged him to pick me up, but everything was so overwhelming that before he got to the studio I ran into the bushes and started crying. I woke up in my bed about twenty hours later with no pants on and a mouth as dry as the Sahara. I never said I made great decisions all the time.

When I came back the next day, I noticed a couple problems: 1) We had run out of time to finish the song, and 2) we had never recorded a bridge and Kesha had already left for tour. If there was ever a time to give up, that would have been a pretty good one. Instead, I took some of the existing vocals from the second verse and reworked them into a bridge. If you listen to the finished song, you'll realize I took her saying "DJ turn it up," repeated it, pitched it, and stretched it as much as I could to make it work. The funny part is that most people tell me it's their favorite part of the song.

Did that situation need to be that difficult? Probably not. But you don't always have a choice. Even if you do, you might make the wrong one. You can look up at the scoreboard, see that you're down by thirty points with a minute left in the game and decide that it's over. Or you can forget about the previous forty-seven minutes and make the most of the sixty seconds that you do have. Assuming we're not really talking about basketball here, there's a really good chance that you'll wind up with something even better than you started with.

No matter how lost or depressed you are or how frustrated you've gotten with not seeing the results you want, there's always a way out. For me, that's getting your hands on one of those little light-up tube things that Will Smith had in *Men in Black* to erase your mind. And if you can't find one of those, take a deep breath, eat an entire large pizza on your couch, and fall asleep in your sweatpants. Then wake up tomorrow and try again.

But I also get it if you're not built quite like I am. When it comes to letting things slide, a duck's back has nothing on me. I get that that's not the norm and that sometimes the negative voices in your head might get a little louder than a pizza and a nap can handle. So I asked the wisest person in my life, my wife, how she handles moving on after failure. Here's what she had to say:

> I've disappointed people. I've disappointed myself. And when I do, I can get stuck in a cycle of repetitive rumination on what and how I could have done better. It's difficult for me to have a healthy relationship with my thoughts. I talk negatively to myself, saying I'm a piece of shit, that it's my fault that I didn't do everything I could have. But when I let those voices win, then every day I'm living in fear of failure, which is truly the scariest thing because that anticipation is worse than anything real that could happen. I've found that the best way to dissipate that lingering feeling is to put my whole heart into something—being the best friend I can be, being the best wife I can be, checking in with people I love. I know it reinforces that cliché idea that there's no such thing as a selfless good deed because a piece of you feels good doing it, but that's what helps me replace those damaging thoughts with affirming ones. *I can get that part, I can do this job, I can live my life to the fullest.* I can't *not* do that. And taking

risks plays a big part. I don't feel like I'm living in my purpose if I'm not taking risks. Honestly, I'd be dead if I didn't take risks in my life. So if and when I do fail, I take the time to mourn any decisions that I made that I might regret; then I connect with my purpose and sense of self and the wholeness that comes from that, and I move forward.

Overnight Success Is a Decade in the Making

A big part of dominating failure is patience. Ninety percent of people who are trying to make it to the same places as you are going to give up because it doesn't happen right away.

I made that number up. But it's a lot. Because most people see the acceptance speeches at the Grammys and the 25 million singles sold and they want that *right now*. Anything else feels like too much time and effort.

Purely by you hustling, grinding, continuing to dust yourself off, and sometimes just riding it out, your competition is going to slip away. If there's one thing I've learned during my time in the music industry, it's that you don't know when things are gonna get good. You don't know when your next song is going to pop. You don't know when your phone is going to ring. Most of the time you don't even get to know when you walk into the studio if things are going to be good because sometimes the music is bad. Okay, not bad, but not great.

Well, you don't *get* to know. So the only way you find out is by continuing to show up.

And you know how *I* know that? Because I know about all the sweat and heartbreak and acid reflux that went into those Grammy nominations and millions of copies sold. You've seen me standing at the top of the mountain, but you didn't see all the toes I lost to frostbite and the dead people I had to eat in order to stay alive.

Remember how I asked Ed Sheeran if I could use the demo we'd been working on for myself and he said yes? Well, that's the only immediate yes in this entire story.

Now, Ed's a baby angel. But when I asked if he wanted to feature on my song as an artist, he said no. He was about to put out an album and a new single and he didn't want to confuse listeners by putting out another song at the same time.

I started thinking about who else I could get on the song. I asked Halsey's management if they could put her on the song. Noncommittal. It goes nowhere. Six months go by.

I'm in the studio with Halsey working on a song called "Now or Never." We're on a lunch break and I play her the demo as she walks back in the room. She loves it. Records her vocals on the spot. *Yes!* It's all starting to happen. Kind of.

I still needed a male vocalist on the song, so I ask Justin Bieber. No answer.

I record Tory Lanez on the song. But he already has a song that's playing on radio, and Interscope's radio department doesn't want to have two different records going out at once. He's out.

I ask Khalid if he wants to be on the song. He says yes, but he's on tour. He records his verse in Germany and sends it to me. I now have everyone on the song. I'm cheering.

I started to put the finishing touches on the song. I changed a few of the vocal parts on Khalid's verse and edited them a little differently than he recorded them to make them sound closer to the original demo. I altered some of the melodies and made some of the words more on top of the beat. Then I sent it to him for his approval.

He hated it. And he said he won't do the song unless I put it back exactly how he originally performed it. I send it back. No answer.

Weeks later, he calls me and says that after living with the song he'd rather record the whole thing again. The only problem is that he's not going to be in town for months. We've already waited like eight months, what's another few? We get to that point in time, I record his vocals. We're excited.

Now we're figuring out how we're going to release this song. As if that wasn't hard enough, in the music business, a lot of musicians will do anything for you in the moment, and then their lawyers and managers and labels come in and destroy everything. An artist might be in an album cycle, so they have other songs they need released instead. The label might want too much of the percentage of the song. Sometimes the label or the manager or the lawyer is in negotiations with another artist's label or manager or lawyer and might be using this as leverage and kill your entire song over something that has nothing to even do with you but you're caught in the crossfire. In any case, there's a good chance that your song will never see the light of day.

Eventually, we make a deal and come to terms with Halsey and Khalid.

A week later, I get a call. Khalid's team changes the entire deal and presents brand-new terms. Halsey hears about those terms and changes hers to match. So now we're back at square one. Somehow, after tons of phone calls, stall tactics, and lawyers yelling at each other, the deal is done. We're finally at the finish line. I send the final around to everyone. The song is scheduled to come out in a week or two.

Khalid says he doesn't like his vocals and wants to record it again.

We have seven days until the song comes out at this point. Which means that the master, or the version that's due to the label, is three days overdue because the digital streaming platforms need the song early enough to ingest it into the software. Meanwhile, months earlier we'd given the song to other territories so they could hear it and come up with a plan for putting it out in their own countries, and I'm petrified that they're going to accidentally put out the old version and Khalid will pull the whole thing down.

We record it again. We get it done. It becomes my first top-ten single on the Billboard Hot 100 as an artist and the longest climb to number one of any song in radio history.

This is just *one* of my stories. Almost everything I do has one just like this attached to it. Roadblocks are guaranteed to happen. Setbacks are guaranteed to happen. Random terrible things are guaranteed to happen. They happen to everybody. You're not special, remember?

The difference between you and everybody else, though, is that you're not going to give up. Because you know that if you do, then it's over. No one's holding your place in line. In fact, there's a whole bunch of other people reading this book right now who will happily take that place from you. So buckle up, stay in it, and I'll see you on the other side.

Maybe It's Not Right Now

Sometimes part of the hustle is knowing when to back up for a minute. It's recognizing that—just like with the songwriting process—you sometimes have to wait for inspiration to come.

It's natural to want to bang your head against the wall and never give up until a) someone finally gets it, or b) you completely knock yourself out.

I've given you at least twenty examples of how I'm normally going full Kool-Aid Man, ramming myself through any obstacle. But that's not always the solution. If you're running up against resistance, the right call could be taking a step back and revisiting an idea later.

Rick Rubin once told me that a great song can be played on any instrument in any key. It doesn't matter because it's a great song no matter what. It's gonna stand the test of time and circumstance. I believe that. That's why I also believe that for any truly good idea, whether it's an invention or a clothing line or a book or a restaurant, there's a time and a place. It's not a question of whether you're gonna find that time and place, just when. So sometimes the most powerful thing you can do is exercise the art of restraint. Restraint from trying to jam an idea into a moment when it's not the right time. Trying to make something work when it's not ready to work.

I have hard drives upon hard drives full of songs that just haven't met their moment yet. It's incredible music. I have songs from being in the studio with Billie Eilish when she was fourteen years old. I have tons of unreleased Juice WRLD songs. SZA songs. A Kendrick Lamar and Ed Sheeran duet. I'll be making a song, and I know it's a great song, but it just hasn't found its home yet. I'm not gonna just throw those things away. I'm not gonna think, *Man, if an artist doesn't want to do something with this then it's total garbage and I've failed.* No, I think, *Maybe it's just not right now.*

So I put them away. Because I know that if something's good, it's gonna have its time. Sometimes that means dressing it up a little or producing it differently, reimagining it, sampling it. But until I know exactly what that should look like,

I file it under "big successes that haven't happened yet." And then every so often, I'll get a feeling in my gut, when inspiration hits or the circumstances are right, and I'll know that it's time to revisit it.

Take Maroon 5 and "Animals." I made that demo five years before it was released. The producer and songwriter Shellback and I originally made the beat and chorus reference for an artist named B.o.B. But, like with most songs you pitch to an artist or label, it didn't work out. Just wasn't the right fit at that time, I guess. So we tabled it. But eventually, we were working with Maroon 5 and looking for scraps of songs that may fit their new project they were working on, and we got the wild idea to take that demo and work on it for them. That's so often how it works—the idea you least expect an artist would be drawn to is the one they get most excited about.

Then there's Kasing Lung. He was working as a children's book illustrator. It was a job that made sense because when he was seven and had moved to the Netherlands from Hong Kong and didn't speak a word of Dutch, a teacher gave him picture books to learn. His career didn't take off, and in his spare time, he doodled creepy little rabbit creatures with sharp teeth inspired by Nordic folklore. In 2015, those creatures became dolls that no one really cared about. In 2019, those dolls were licensed by a giant Chinese toy company. In 2024, Lisa from BLACKPINK posted about the creepy rabbit dolls. A-list celebrities want them. Fashion designers feature them as part of their collections. Brands like Coca-Cola and Olive Garden want in on collaborations. By summer 2025, you couldn't scroll two posts on TikTok or Instagram without seeing someone posting about their Labubus, which have generated billions of dollars of revenue. All because Kasing Lung didn't give up on his creepy little rabbit sketches.

Look at Bruno Mars. Lady Gaga. Katy Perry. All signed young. All had failed careers. Dropped from labels. Broke. Slammed by critics. All came back again at a different time, and now they're some of the biggest names in music. Charli xcx is another great example. When I first met her, she was thirteen or fourteen years old and supposed to be the next big thing. She was writing songs for herself and other people and was having some success, but then it kind of stalled out. Something just wasn't connecting for her. She finally got tired of listening to her label about the music they wanted her to make and made songs that she loved, which was this weird, left-of-center sound. It didn't initially pan out, but it did create a cult fan base. And then, *years* later, *Brat* happened.

Everything in life is about timing. My relationship with Selena is another great example. We first met about fifteen years ago. We worked together five or six years after that, and then again five or six years after that, and had a casual friendship during that time. *Then* we started dating a few years after that. And now she's my wife. We always talk about how it never would have worked out if it were at a different time or place in our lives because neither one of us would likely have been ready. As twentysomethings we were still kids. We hadn't had enough therapy. We weren't equipped to deal with the issues. We both needed to fail a bunch of times in other relationships to know what we really needed and to know our worth. And now we do.

Sometimes the world isn't ready for you. Sometimes you're not ready for the world. When I was sixteen and I'd go play people my beats but they wouldn't take anything, I'd ask anyone who would listen, "Why aren't they into my beats? I'm good enough—I'm great, I'm amazing." But looking back at it, *I* wasn't ready. From a technical standpoint, I *wasn't* good enough yet. The world was telling me that I needed more time to hone my craft.

Don't get me wrong—it's hard to wait. It's hard to be patient. You're talking to a guy who still gets third-degree burns on the roof of his mouth from eating too-hot pizza. You're probably going to hear a voice in your head saying that it might never happen. Or that the opportunity has passed. Or that you're not good enough. Or some other garbage that you know isn't true because it's lame and you're not lame. Which is when you know you've got to 1) be nice to yourself and learn how to get out of your own head (which we're getting to eventually, but if you have the impulse control of a fruit fly you can go right to page 169) and 2) double down on trusting your gut.

Trust Your Gut

Ammar Malik and I had recorded a demo for a song called "Stereo Hearts." We'd put Gym Class Heroes on it, but we were stuck on who could sing the chorus. Ammar's manager, David Silberstein, suggested Adam Levine. Maroon 5 was obviously huge at this point, but they weren't as poppy as they once were. So I thought it was a cool idea to put him on the song because it would be unexpected. It made me think of Train and "Hey, Soul Sister," which had just been a big hit for them. A lot of people thought I was crazy.

When you do a song with someone, you have to jump through so many hoops and get so many people to agree before it comes out. But I knew this would work, so I kept pushing. I hadn't even asked Adam if he would do the chorus at this point. He'd never written with someone else, and he definitely had never sung someone else's lyrics. So I told him that he could make changes and make it feel more like his own style. He agreed to give it a shot. But then when we were in the studio, he liked how he sounded on the chorus so much that he tried to hijack the whole song and make it a Maroon 5 record. He begged for it. I had to think fast.

I said to him, "Dude, don't worry; I have an even bigger song for you to get on for yourself!" It was complete bullshit. And he was so stoked that he made me open my calendar on the spot to plan our next session for the following week to work on this mythical "bigger song." Which meant I had five days to make a hit song appear out of thin air.

I'm wracking my brain, calling everyone I know to send me even a kernel of an idea. I was on FaceTime with Shellback, aka Johan, and we were going through a bunch of rough ideas he had started but nothing was hitting me. Right as he was about to hang up, he said, "I have this one other little thing but haven't really played it for anyone." He pressed play; I heard the opening whistle, the guitar riff that sounded like Jamiroquai, and I felt like I was gonna have a heart attack—it was everything I wanted and more. We started making a demo back and forth between Sweden and LA. I flew out Ammar from Virginia to work on it. All of this happened within a few days. We got a solid but wonky demo to play for Adam—he loved it. We worked on it for a week straight. In the demo, Johan had this gibberish melody that sounded like "I got the moves like Jagger," so we made that the concept of the song. Even if you didn't know who Mick Jagger was, it sounded cool.

Before we knew it, Adam's vocals were done, and once we incorporated all the band's live instruments, the song really felt like it was alive. When I'm making a song, there is a moment where it all clicks, everything is working, and we have this song that we all love. It's done. We had that moment.

I played Jordi the finished song and he started screaming. At first I thought he was mad, but then I realized that he was so excited about the song that all he could do was yell at the top of his lungs. After he caught his breath, he began to tell me about this new TV show that Adam was going to be a judge on called *The Voice*. He said, "It's like *American Idol*." And I looked at him and said, "But there already is an *American Idol*?" And he immediately launched into a sales pitch on why this was going to crush *American Idol* and any other show like it. I thought he was full of shit, but fine.

He then told me there's a performance portion at the end of every show and that the next week's slot was Adam's. The only problem was that they were scheduled to perform a song they had at radio called "Never Gonna Leave This Bed." Jordi had an idea to switch which song they would be performing without telling the label and play "Moves like Jagger" instead (and release it at the same time). They did it, and all of our phones were ringing off the hook. The label was beyond pissed. But I went to bed, and when I woke up, the song was number one in more than eighty-five countries.

Anyways, we wound up finishing "Stereo Hearts" and successfully pulling a bait and switch on Adam, and both songs were hits. It was the beginning of such a great music-making relationship with Maroon 5 because we believed in each other and trusted each other. Ammar went from making a demo in his parents' basement to having two Billboard number ones five months later. And everyone was betting against us. A lot of people thought we were crazy to put Adam as a feature on "Stereo Hearts" because Maroon 5 had been moving away from the Top 40 pop mainstream and people weren't playing bands anymore. I didn't give a fuck because I felt the magic, and sometimes that's all it takes. Even when everyone else is saying no. We believed in our instincts and trusted our process, so the rest was just noise.

The moral of the story is that you have to trust your gut, even if you're wrong in the end. Because if you learn from that, then there's no such thing as wrong, just back to the drawing board and coming back bigger, faster, stronger. Your gut is your secret weapon. It goes back to that little investigation you conducted a few sections back. The one where you thought about what makes you unique. Where you thought about the stuff that makes you different from anyone else out there, even the people trying to do the exact same thing you are. The stuff that makes your shitty haircut the one that everyone's going to be lining up to get in a few years. *You* are the one part of this whole equation that makes whatever dream you're chasing viable. Because no one can do it the way you do. And at the end of the day, *no one knows* what the right answer is. For real. So you might as well go with the one that feels right.

Stay Stoked

As effective as it is for me, "work hard and don't give up" is the least sexy thing you can tell someone to do. It even sounds annoying. Sorry.

You think an NBA player wants to go to practice every single day and shoot a hundred of the same shot? You think people getting their PhD want to sit at home working on thesis papers and advanced calculus when they could be doing literally anything else?

There are going to be some days when you hit a nice, smooth patch of road and all that work you're putting in feels easy. But most of the time, it's gonna be days when the rubber treads are worn down to the rims, you're out of gas, and you have to pee. That's when you have to find a way to stay inspired. To keep things fun. To be your own biggest cheerleader, even when there's nothing to cheer about.

Whenever I find myself waking up and not being excited about what I'm doing for the day, it's a problem for me. It's a problem because the second we start going through the motions, the second we lose touch with the hunger that's driving us to do this in the first place, everyone around us can feel it. If you're not stoked, they're not going to be stoked. It doesn't matter who "they" is in this scenario—all that matters is that no one's gonna be buying what you're selling, which is the whole point of all that boulder pushing anyway. Whenever that happens, here's what I do:

Shake it up. Sometimes it's as simple as breaking up the day. I don't know about you, but I can't do anything for more than thirty minutes straight. Sitting around all day hyperfocused on something is probably going to drive you nuts. So break it up. Go for a walk. Eat a snack. Eat another snack. Make yourself lunch. I like to have something in my mouth as a little activity, so I keep loose food in my pocket like a squirrel, nuts or candies that have little lint balls and hairs on them that I have to blow off before eating them. Or if you don't have any of these choices because you have to be in a cubicle all day and getting out of your chair is the difference between life and death—which I have a hard time believing, unless you're a surgeon, in which case, by all means carry on—I think you can figure something out. Throw a little desk party if you get through thirty minutes of cleaning out your email. Turn and talk to your neighbor. Turn off your monitor for a few minutes to rest your eyeballs. Read the next chapter of this book.

Press pause. There are going to be days when you wake up and can't even bring yourself to look at that boulder. Maybe you've been beaten down for a week or a month or six months straight and you're exhausted or you're getting hit from too many angles by too many problems. The first thing I do any time I'm feeling overwhelmed by a problem I can't see a solution to is I stand up. Like literally get the fuck up. And then I take a step back. An actual step. I take a deep breath. I take a sip of water. I go for a walk. (A lot of the same things I'm going to recommend when it comes to getting out of your head, which believe me, we're getting to.) Then I see if I can get more of an aerial view of the problem. Sometimes that takes five minutes. Other times it can take the whole day. Or a week. Or a month. I give myself permission to get that space because 1) there's no point in continuing to grind through a problem you have no idea how to solve, and 2) it's the kind of rest I know that I need in order to keep my little stool steady. To keep my work feeling fresh. To keep the creativity flowing. Then, when I've had a chance to catch my breath and figure things out, I get back in there and keep pushing. File it under "stupid-sounding things that actually work."

Go back to your why. To stay inspired, I revisit the original reason of why I'm doing all this in the first place. When I connect to that honest, soulful place that got me so stoked on day one—five-year-old me chasing the music and how understood and free it made me feel—the hype follows. It's way too easy to get wrapped up in the why-nots—why something didn't work, why we're not as good as another person, why we're not seeing the success we thought we would—but focusing on the why, or why you're going after this thing that you're passionate about and want to keep doing, is kryptonite against that. Generally, for me, my why is because something makes me happy. Because it makes me feel good. Of course there are parts about the process of getting there that I can't stand and that I'm losing sleep and pulling my hair out and losing my mind over, but when I realize that I love what I do and that all that frustrating stuff is the byproduct of getting to do that, then I get a little more gratitude in my attitude.

Take a left turn. This goes back to the power of getting lost. If the hill that you're pushing that boulder up seems like it's only getting taller and steeper and there's no top in sight, take a little off-road detour. When writing songs kept taking me to dead ends, I started a record label. When my creativity for making music doesn't feel as juicy as it should, I take out something else I've been working on and push that boulder up a hill for a while. No one said you only have to have one boulder.

And if all else fails, and work just feels like work, the best thing you can do is go back to the basics: Shut up. Dream big. Work hard. And don't, under any circumstances, be a dick about it.

c[redacted]er

5

Don't Be a Dick.

I wasn't sure if I needed an entire chapter just to tell you not to be an asshole, but here we are. It's sort of the whole reason I wanted to write this book in the first place—because, to me, success is not only accomplishing the things you aimed high for, but also knowing that you didn't step on a single other person along the way to get there. Now that I think about it, this entire book should have just been called *Don't Be a Dick*.

I know it sounds like an obvious concept, but you'd be amazed by how many people are just huge jerks. Or maybe you wouldn't be. It's always so surprising to me because being nice doesn't take any effort. I can't really tell you how the human body works, but wouldn't you believe me if I told you that it takes more physical and mental effort to be mean to someone than to just show up and treat them with kindness? Telling a coworker that you see how hard they're hustling and that you're proud of them? Telling your partner when they open their eyes in the morning how beautiful/handsome they are and how grateful you are to spend the rest of your life with them? Telling a friend how much they mean to you? These little things take a *second* out of our day but could make someone's entire week. Our words have so much weight and value. I'm still holding on to things my parents said to me when I was six. Positive and negative. So you can imagine how what you say to your kids/your boss/your assistant/that guy calling to schedule your oil change/your partner/your friends affects them. And I don't know about you, but I live in a world where what you put out, you get back.

This is yet another lesson from the Sandy Levin playbook. My mother is one of the kindest, most selfless people I've ever met. If only 10 percent of her rubbed off on me, what a blessing. I always wonder how she turned out to be such a good person because her mother was an asshole. Maybe the top three meanest people to exist, sandwiched between Hitler and Stalin. She never once said "I love you" to my mom when she was alive. But my mom made sure she said it to me not only every day, but way too many times throughout the day. I was smothered with love. And she sacrificed so much for me, taking me to studios until 2 a.m., traveling up and down the East Coast for meetings that never panned out. What my mom taught me was that it doesn't cost anything to be nice. Or to be a good person. And that it goes such a long way in lifting up everyone else around you.

That doesn't have to change in order to become successful. Or after you become successful.

I've been able to accomplish so many things in my life and still be kind. Are there a few people in the world who might say differently? I guess. But in the twenty-three years I've been working in music and on so many different types of projects—film, TV, books—I'd say that 95 percent of the people I've done that with will tell you that I'm a good guy who put his morals and values first. Whoever wrote that nice guys finish last is an idiot. And wrong.

When you show up for other people the way you'd want them to show up for you, when you set people up to do their best, everybody wins. The creativity flows better. The ideas get better. And the success definitely tastes sweeter.

You don't win any points by making people feel terrible. The only thing you do get is lonely and sad. And what are we doing if we don't have anyone to share our success with? If you've made it to the top but you've alienated everyone around you and have no one left who actually likes you for you, what the fuck are you doing? Was it worth it to make $25 million in a year but all your children hate you? Remember the stool. You fail in one area, you fail in all areas. Success is when *everyone* is winning.

Eric André once asked me to do a live performance version of his television show. I go onstage in front of thousands of people, and I have to chug all these different things. First was a beer. I hate beer. Nobody should drink beer. It makes no sense; it just gets you full. Second was a Red Bull. The only other time I tasted Red Bull was when I was thirteen at my brother's fraternity and it had vodka in it. Equally as disgusting as beer. Third was the hottest hot sauce in the world.

Somehow, during all the chugging and messing around, I got sauce in my eye. I didn't want to break character, but the burning was getting so intense I basically had to disassociate. Five or six minutes later, I come to and I'm crowd surfing. Everything was pretty much a blur after that, but I wound up vomiting in a bathroom, covered in ice water because I had burns all over my face, and then was rushed to the hospital.

It was the night before Selena's birthday, and I was supposed to be relaxing with her in Malibu instead of heat-stroking out in my own vomit. At around 1:30 a.m., I called to let her know what had happened, and before I even hung up, she had already left her friends that she was with to come to the hospital. An hour and a half away.

She took care of me all night, then drove back in the early morning so no one even noticed she was gone. She never brought up the situation, and nobody ever knew except the two of us. And now you. She's the true definition of a ride or die. The embodiment of what it means to put someone else first in your relationship, even if it means coming to the hospital on your birthday 'cuz your husband ate too much hot sauce and pooped in his pants.

That's just *one* of my relationships. I am lucky enough to have that same level of security and support with a ton of people in my life, in personal *and* professional relationships. And it happens to pay some serious dividends.

What's Your ROI?

If I opened my phone right now, scrolled to a random number, and dialed in the middle of the night because I shit myself, there's like an 85 percent chance that that person would show up for me with a spare change of clothes. That number is only so low because the other 15 percent are numbers for people I probably haven't talked to since high school. But even they might consider jumping into their cars because I've always made it my mission to treat everyone like *I* would do the same thing for them. It's the right thing to do.

Let's play a game: It's 3 a.m. Your car broke down and you're an hour and fifteen minutes from home. How many people can you call who will come pick you up at the drop of a hat, no questions asked? If no one comes to mind, that's a bummer. That should maybe get you thinking about what you're prioritizing. Or how nice of a person you've been. But if you're struggling to pick just one single person from a super long list of people who would hands-down show up for you, that's what I call being rich. That's what I call being successful. That you've gotten to a place in your life where you can count on people and they can count on you.

In business, they call that an ROI—return on investment. The more you invest in your relationships, the more you're gonna get back.

My friend Julia Michaels is an incredible songwriter. In 2015, she had just started to get big and had a few hits under her belt. She cowrote "Sorry" with Justin Bieber. The day that song came out and went number one, she came into the studio. We surprised her with champagne and cupcakes, and she was smiling . . . and then she was crying. I mean, I thought champagne and cupcakes were nice, but not *that* nice. She was happy about the accomplishment, but she told us that she had also just broken up with her boyfriend and was having a hard time keeping it together. We talked about life for a while, though mostly about how much of a dickhead her ex was. I thought there was no way we would write a song that day, but when I suggested she maybe try to write one about her current situation to make her feel better, she agreed. Then she walked into the control room with me, Justin Tranter, and Tor Hermansen and Mikkel Eriksen, producers and songwriters known as Stargate.

I'd been wanting to do one of those songs that has an orchestra behind it, like Jazmine Sullivan's "Bust Your Windows" or Rihanna's "Unfaithful." So we start messing around with some string sounds and Julia starts humming the chorus melody, and the song basically just fell out of the sky into our laps. It just happened so quickly. We were all in awe. Sometimes you can't tell if a song is good when you're writing it—not with this one. We were grinning from ear to ear. We sent it around to some people and it was like drugs; everyone was addicted. Every label, A&R, artist, and manager was trying to snag it for something.

Julia called me a few days later and said, "benny, I think I want to become an artist, and I think I want to use this song. It's the first time I've ever written a song that sounds so much like myself, and I could never picture anyone else singing it—it's too personal." I was all for it. I believed in her so much as a songwriter and as a person that if she felt something deep in her soul, then it must be gospel.

Some of our surrounding teams didn't share that vision. Julia didn't even have a record deal at that point, and some of the biggest artists in the world were begging to record the song. There were many arguments, rude emails, hung-up phone calls around this thing. But I kept helping her push it over the finish line to becoming the first song she released as a solo artist.

When "Issues" came out . . . it connected. Like a motherfucker. That year, Julia got nominated for Best New Artist *and* Song of the Year at the Grammys. But it so easily could have been another artist's song. Is it cool to have a huge artist taking on one of your projects? For sure. But being an advocate for a friend and then getting to be involved in breaking a new artist with so much personality and sense of self and introducing them to the world is so much better than that ever could be.

Your relationships should function the same way. They shouldn't be based on what another person can do for you. It should not be tit for tat. There shouldn't be a hierarchy in your contacts based on people's success. It should be based on how you treat one another and the general understanding that you're going to be there for one another.

Sound a little too warm and fuzzy for you? Picture the top of that stool, the success that rests on top of your work, your health, and your relationships. That's where you want to park yourself eventually. But think that's gonna be able to handle your big, juicy behind if that relationship leg is nothing but ego and burned bridges? There's no such thing as making up for it with a double-wide Career leg. I tried. It sucked.

So be nice. Money, opportunity, business—that will all come. But first, you gotta get the fuck out of your own way. Yet again.

Check Your Ego

Seriously. Get over yourself. When you check your ego and your own bullshit, you get the best out of everyone around you. And that leads to success, for everyone involved, in every meaning of the word.

I've built an entire career on doing exactly that. More than anything else I do, getting the best out of people is the number one goal, and setting ego aside is the first requirement. Consider what an average writing session in the studio looks like:

First, you have the artist. They walk into the room, and in their head, their idea is correct either 100 percent of the time or zero percent of the time, depending on their confidence level that day. Then you might have one or two producers. Maybe one or two songwriters. And each of these people thinks *they're* right most of the time too. On top of all that, you might have a songwriter who is working with a huge artist for the first time and this might be their big break, so they feel like their whole life is riding on this session. One of the producers could be a big deal and so they feel all this pressure because everything they do is expected to go number one. The artist has to have this song done in the next five hours because the album is due in the next two weeks because their entire tour is pegged to that and that's going to dictate the next eighteen months of their life. And then you have me, who has to deliver on all of the above. Geez, I'm getting a little anxious just thinking about this.

What I know is that beyond writing and producing a great song, my most important job is to balance everyone's opinions, feelings, and expectations. So the first thing I do is get us all loosened up and comfortable so we can let our guards down. Namely because we need to be able to say exactly how we're feeling so we can figure out what to write a song about. Remember, sometimes I'm meeting some of these people for the first time, and I have to somehow get them to trust me within minutes of walking into the room. I usually do this with a combination of dick and fart jokes, storytelling, dumb YouTube videos, or, if you're SZA, a tray of banana pudding.

Then, let's say the artist wants to write a song about heartbreak and everyone gets super excited about it. Well, everyone in the room has their own version of heartbreak. I then have to find a way to weave together everyone's thoughts and opinions in a cohesive statement. Maybe Songwriter One has the best idea in the room. I might hear what they have to say and know it's right, but I want the artist to get their feelings out first. So I might have to sit on that idea for a little while, then circle back around with it but in a way so Songwriter One doesn't get upset that I'm not leading with it and the artist doesn't get upset that they didn't come up with it, all while Songwriter Two is coming up with their idea. It's a balancing act of making everybody around me feel heard and respected because if someone doesn't feel respected, they're gonna be upset; it's gonna change the vibe of the room; and then nothing gets accomplished.

"Vibe" is a corny way to say it, but that's really what it all comes down to—you have to keep the vibe right. You have to think about what other people are thinking and feeling and let them feel seen and heard too. That goes for personal relationships, business relationships—whether it's between you and a partner or you and the three hundred people who work for you—and at home with your family. That can't happen if your head is stuck three feet up the inside of your own ass.

The sooner you realize it's not all about you, the quicker you're gonna get where you want to go. Because now *everyone's* on your team. And sometimes—or in my case, a lot of the time—other people can be better than you at some things. Or have the better idea. Which means that when you're not too busy shutting them down so you can show them how big your dick is, you're getting to take advantage of that. If I'm running a session and Jimi Hendrix were alive and in the studio laying down a guitar line, I'm not gonna take the guitar from Jimi and say, "I've got it from here."

Okay, maybe not the best example, but I really liked it when I first thought of it. How about one of your junior associates has a great concept for something you've been working on and pitches it in a meeting you're running? Or your four-year-old comes up with what should be for dinner? The best idea wins. Period. No matter where it comes from.

There will always be someone smarter, better, and younger than you. You could waste all your time and energy thinking of all the reasons why you shouldn't like them, or you could join forces with them. If I tried to do what I do on my own or didn't listen to other people's ideas, I'd a) make really shitty music and b) not be writing this book because no one would want to work with me ever. Look at the credits for any song or movie or television show—the people whose names are the biggest and boldest are usually thanking a lot of other people who helped them along the way. And chances are that their thing would never have been as great as it is if they hadn't listened to each of those people to some extent. Sure, there's plenty of ego-hyped narcissists in my industry and every single other one. But I've lived my life by these words, and they've served me well.

In 2011, I was in the studio with Mikkel and Tor, aka Stargate. We were working on some music and going for a Lana Del Rey vibe but wound up making something that would work for Eminem or Kanye. We sent it to Paul Rosenberg, Eminem's manager, who loved it and said he was sending it to him. Months and months went by and we never heard back. (This is very common in the music business.) One day, Sia was in the studio. She had finished a bunch of demos for the day and called a car to pick her up. The dispatcher told her it would be a twenty-five-minute wait (this was before Uber), so she said, "Pull up another beat and I'll write to it while I wait." Mikkel pressed play on the beat we had sent to Eminem, and in fifteen minutes we had the lyrics, melody, harmonies, full song completely done. (And she still had a few minutes to use the restroom before her car arrived.) We named the demo "Diamonds in the Sky."

At this point, Stargate said, "We're gonna send this to Rihanna." And I told them I didn't think the song was strong enough or the right fit. I thought we had some other demos that might suit her more. Tor told me how they had like ten Billboard number ones with Rihanna and that I just needed to trust him. And that he was going to send it even if I said no, which I continued to do because I thought it was a bad idea. He sent it.

She loved it. She loved it so much that she wanted to record it the next day while she was in London.

When she was in the studio recording the song, Ty-Ty Smith, cofounder of Roc Nation, had the idea to take the "shine bright like a diamond" section that was only the bridge and put it on top of the second half of the chorus, which made the song ten thousand times catchier.

I still remember being in ABC Carpet & Home in New York with Sia when we got an email from Roc Nation saying that Rihanna had recorded the song the night before and that it was going to come out in two days. *Wait, what?!* This all happened within a few days of its inception. We sat on a couch in the store and listened to the song over and over again. Meanwhile, I'd had a meeting the week before with Def Jam, the label Rihanna's signed to, where they'd told me that they were looking for songs to release the following *year*. They were completely clueless!

"Diamonds" came out, became an instant classic and one of Rihanna's career-defining records, and it was because of all the people who touched it and shaped it along the way. If I hadn't gotten past my ego and allowed that to happen, that song would have never happened. You have to let go and listen to the people around you because you're not always right. You have to put your pride and ego aside, or at the very least go for a ride and see what happens. Because you'll be rewarded if you do.

As for Eminem, Paul Rosenberg eventually called me back just before "Diamonds" hit the radio to say that Eminem loves the beat and wanted to do something to it. I had to let him down gently—even though I hadn't heard from him in a year—and let him know that Rihanna was putting out the song any day now. So I guess this story is kind of a twofer because the takeaway is also that you should take advantage of an opportunity when you see one.

Learning how to collaborate, in life and in love, is like creating a good-idea factory. The best suggestions will always make it through because you're letting everyone have a say and not getting in their way. Even the terrible suggestions, when not immediately shut down, could one day become the best suggestions. Because if you don't make Susan feel dumb for making one not-so-great contribution, then she'll feel confident enough to keep putting up shots until she's the one with the buzzer-beater. Nice work, Susan. Or maybe that truly terrible idea from a moment ago sparks genius in someone else, which leads to the perfect answer to your problem. But that can only happen when you stop believing that you're the only one with the good ideas.

There's Enough Cake

You also need to get past the idea that a win for someone else is one less win for you. Hear me when I tell you: There's enough success in this world for everyone to have some. The cake is *so big*. It's big enough for everybody to get full to the point that they get another roll under their bellies and their faces hurt from the sugar high.

I've lost mentors over the idea that if someone takes a slice it means one less slice for them. That's why when it comes to my own mentoring, I embrace the idea of setting people free—they don't have to be under my tutelage forever. It's okay for the babies to leave the nest, spread their wings, and fly away. And someday, that same baby could come back and help hand me a win. Or build a bigger nest or catch more worms or whatever the fuck it is that birds consider to be a win.

About twelve years ago, I was playing poker at my friend Shelli Azoff's house. She posted a picture of a winning hand during the game, and I happened to be in the background. At the end of the night, she walked up to me and said, "Apparently you are a big deal and my son's friend is obsessed with you and wants to work for you—just make him an intern." I wasn't looking for interns at the time, but she was so convincing that I set up a meeting the next day.

The kid was fifteen years old, barely any hair on his face and probably not his nuts either. He just seemed sweet, and I saw part of myself in him. He ended up working for me every day until he graduated from high school. Then, when he was in college, Ed Sheeran and I convinced his school to let him leave to go on tour with us.

After about four years of working for me, he finally played me his music. I didn't even know he made music. He never even mentioned it to me, but he broke down one night after his therapist gave him an ultimatum: *Play benny your music or I'm gonna stop working with you.* He played me three demos. They were terrible. Borderline unlistenable.

It didn't matter, though. Because I saw something in him called the "It Factor." He may not have been that good in the moment, and he might have been the most forgettable person on that tour, getting people's lunch and coffee orders, but he knew how to speak to people. He knew how to make people feel comfortable, how to disarm them. And that's more important than any musical talent. When you know how to work the room and own it, any skill set is secondary. So I went against everything I should probably have done in that moment and I signed him.

His name is Blake Slatkin, and you might have heard of him because over the next few years, he worked his ass off, had a bunch of number one hit songs like "Stay" by The Kid LAROI and Justin Bieber and "Unholy" by Sam Smith and Kim Petras, won Grammy record of the year, and became one of my best friends.

Now, I want you to look at how he and Ed and I all invested in our relationships and won big. We didn't owe Blake anything; he didn't owe us anything. But our karmic energy paid us back tenfold. And if I could take a minute to pat myself on the back, a big part of that was choosing not to be a dick and not getting threatened about the fact that someone who was younger or less experienced than me could not only succeed, but also work with the same artists.

Blake's being successful actually has nothing to do with me, just like your coworker or friend or social media nemesis's success has nothing to do with you. It doesn't mean you're any less talented or worthy. It just means that they have something unique and special. And you do too. *Awww.*

So yeah, you want to win big? Or better yet, you want to know that when you fall flat on your face there's going to be a team of people waiting there to pick you back up? Then you have to be nice. Considering that I just made you make a list of the biggest, hardest, hairiest goals you could possibly accomplish and I'm telling you that being a good person is a huge piece of how you get there, I'm hoping this isn't too crazy of an ask. Especially because, if we're being honest, you really only have to do the bare minimum.

Do the Bare Minimum

Here's some great news (I guess?): The bar for being a decent person and making people feel seen and heard and cared for is really low. I know this because in an interview with Jay Shetty for his podcast, I told him about some of the things I do for Selena in our relationship. Things like checking in on her, being emotionally available, letting her know I'm thinking about her. Giving her a heads-up if I'm going to be home late. Telling her "I love you" before bed because I know that means something to her. We're talking the bare minimum kind of stuff that one person can do for another, especially someone they love. And the internet went *crazy*. That interview was shared millions of times. The audio went viral with all these people—mostly women—asking if this is some kind of new movement in relationships.

It's not. It's just being nice.

I was lucky to get a master class in relationships, how to treat people, and how to want to be treated from my mom. When she was still married to my dad, I learned that when two people are unhappy in a relationship and have tried so many times to make it work, it's okay to walk away. I also learned compassion, specifically in the form of a woman who was in the process of divorcing her husband while also nursing him through the lows of his mental illness. Then, when I was going through puberty and starting to have my first romantic experiences with girls, I was simultaneously watching my mom dating a whole roster of losers. Guys who would treat her poorly. Nitpick things she did. Cheat on her. Lie to her. Guys who didn't ask the right questions on dates. We were in the trenches together, navigating love at two very different points in life, and yet she was teaching me these incredible lessons on how to be a better partner. More than that—a better man. She taught me the art of listening. The art of picking my battles. The art of valuing what my partner has to say. The art of valuing my partner's imperfections, not trying to fix them. Accepting them as they are. The art of being the yin to their yang. And most importantly, the art of showing my partner their worth and making sure they actually believe it, exactly how she did that for me.

I was once on a friend's podcast, and he asked me what mitzvah I had done lately. Meaning, a good deed or act of kindness. I give money to charity, which is one way I do that, but in that moment, I realized that the real mitzvah that I'm doing every single day is showing up in the lives of people I love. It's checking in on a friend who I know is dealing with something. It's calling my mom when she's having a tough day and listening to everything she has to say (even if sometimes it's going, *Uh-huh, yeah,* for twenty minutes). When I wake up, I think to myself, *How can I make Selena's day better?* Because that makes *my* day better. And Selena does exactly the same thing, thinking, *How can I make benny's day better?* It's give and it's take and it's not a weakness—it's a strength.

That doesn't just apply to the people you're dating or married to. It should be everyone—your kids, your parents, your coworkers, your bosses, whoever is bagging your groceries or cutting your hair or mowing your lawn. Treat everyone the same and everyone well. You think I don't remember how people treated me when I was an intern scrubbing toilets and getting coffee for Disco D? So many of the producers and songwriters and artists I met during that time are still in the industry. Some of them were pieces of shit to me back then but are super nice to me now that I can give them something back. But some of them were really nice to me when I had no perceived value to them; they were just nice out of the kindness of their heart. That's real character, and that goes a long way with me.

All of the above should tell you two things:

1. **Hold your business relationships to the same standards as your personal ones.** Don't sacrifice your value system for making a few extra dollars. It will drain your emotional and health bars down to zero.

   That's why deciding who I'm gonna work with is a big deal. I'm never going into it thinking, *Will we make good music together?* It's *Can we write well together? Will we cook well together? Do I want to have them over for dinner? Do our morals align? Do they understand the importance of family? Do they have a good sense of self? Are they a good person? Are they trying to better themselves and those around them?*

Especially in the beginning of your career, you'll be tempted to say yes to people and relationships that might lead to bigger opportunities down the road—no matter who they are or what they're about. But as I've gotten older, I've realized that it's better to stick to your guns and find great collaborators than to work with people who might give you short-term gains but long-term pain.

2. **Hold your personal relationships to the same standards as your business ones.** If you're going to invest everything into a relationship, make sure they deserve it. Spending all that capital on people who are throwing it away on stupid stuff like being passive-aggressive or not supporting you back is just bad business.

   Think about who you're surrounding yourself with in the first place. For starters, people use the word *friend* way too loosely. *Oh yeah, that's my best friend.* No, it's not. That's Kirk, the guy you met at a bar two and a half weeks ago. He's an acquaintance at best. I feel like calling someone I've known for like eight years a "best friend" is pushing it. Try thirty years. Don't get me wrong, there's a few lifelong soul mates who have snuck through the cracks in less time than that, but they're few and far between.

Second, make sure you value having friends from all different walks of life. I have friends who worked for the Obama administration. I know Taylor Swift. But I also have my friend Lev who works IT at Capital One and helped me get a virus off my computer. In life, in business, and in love, it's all about bonding with people who aren't like you and finding ways to coexist so you can learn to better yourself and to better each other.

I can't believe I'm writing a self-help book. I'm an idiot.

Listen

This probably comes as a surprise to pretty much everybody, but I used to be afraid to speak up. Before my parents got divorced, the idea of voicing my opinion scared me. I felt like if I did say something, no one would hear me because nobody listened to anybody. Or that I'd be belittled or made to feel small.

It made me realize how important it is that everyone in my life feel listened to.

Being patient is the most important part of that. A child coming to you with an idea or a concern or a question is the exact same scenario as, say, an intern at your company or someone who works with you coming to you and wanting to be heard in some way. Or your partner wanting to be heard in some way. They might not know the best way to say it or show it or even have a very good idea in the first place, but what you need to do in that moment, no matter what, is shut up and listen.

I can't tell you how many times I've been in meetings and sessions and conversations where someone is suggesting something and I'm sitting there thinking, *I'm pretty sure that is not correct,* or, *There's no way that'll work.* Not necessarily because I had a better idea but, well, it was just a not-good idea. It happens. God knows I've had plenty of them. But I can't just come out and say that and have that be the starting point. It would shut down the conversation.

Instead, I let that person finish spooling out their idea, and I always respond with encouragement. Or at least not something negative. Because a) sometimes in that exercise they wind up coming up with something that's even better than what they originally put out there. Or anything I would have come up with. And b) cutting someone off before they've finished working through their idea or being a dick about it doesn't make them feel like you care about them. And it definitely doesn't make them want to continue contributing.

When people feel like they can toss out any idea and that no idea is stupid, you start to really learn about the people in your life—what they like, what they need, what makes them feel special. Their strengths and their weaknesses.

As a bonus, you get some great ideas. Like the time I was sitting in my studio writing a song and couldn't come up with the end of the chorus, or what's called the tagline. My friend David Silberstein, who is not a songwriter or producer, was in the other room and shouted out, "What if the last line said, 'Get your ass back home'?" In that moment we all laughed and put it in as a placeholder. But when we tried to beat it, we couldn't. "Ass Back Home" by Gym Class Heroes went on to sell millions of copies. To this day, that's David Silberstein's only credit on a song.

We all love to hear ourselves talk. Current company included. But sometimes it's about quieting down. You know what I hate more than anything? When I can like *hear* someone's lip quivering because they're waiting for me to finish just so they can get to their point. That's just not how you're going to grow your relationships or your trust. So yeah, here I am once again telling you to shut the fuck up.

Conflict Is a Waste of Energy

Say it with me: *Conflict is a waste of energy*.

There are only so many hours in a day. You want to spend them being upset with somebody? Why? Like really ask yourself why. What's the point of holding something against someone that they can't even help, like getting the job you might have wanted or being chosen to do something great that has absolutely nothing to do with you? Whose life is that making better? It's that whole idea of resentment being like drinking poison and hoping the other person bites it.

The same goes for getting into an argument—why even do it? So you can win? Get a trophy for being the smartest, rightest person in the world? If you feel like you need to pummel another person into the ground just so you can feel right, does anyone win? (And are you okay?)

I'm not a pushover, but I try to pick my battles. I only insert my opinion if it's something so important that it needs to be set straight or else it's going to be an issue in the future. When I'm solving a problem or making a decision, I take a big step back and look at whatever it is from all angles. A lot of people are doing that in a 2D model, getting stuck with what's right in front of them. But I'm looking at it in 3D and thinking about what happens ten years from now because of whatever choice I'm making today. Like deciding to take a smaller advance on a new publishing deal in order to get the reversion rights on my songs, which means that someone else doesn't own my songs in perpetuity and I'll eventually have full control over my entire catalog, which I could then sell at some point if that's what I want to do. It was a chess move I made fifteen years ago, sacrificing temporary gains for a bigger long-term payoff. But if something isn't a big deal, then I don't make it a big deal. And the only way you can do that is if you're willing to take yourself out of the equation and realize not everything is about you.

The same goes for this wildly unnecessary need so many of us have to fix every situation immediately. Especially men—why do we have that built into our DNA? Why is someone else having a problem like a flashing green light for us to barrel in and start moving things around? Is it some kind of leftover fantasy of us all wanting to be construction workers when we were three? But we're also not the only ones—I'm looking at anyone who's ever been in an argument with their partner because they were upset about something, and now you're arguing because you made it all about you, and now you're mad about arguing, so now you're arguing about *that*. There's no application process for becoming an adult. I checked.

What you could try instead is what I put into practice in my relationship with Selena. It's called shutting your mouth and giving someone space.

Sometimes she just wants to vent or be frustrated. Sometimes she needs twenty-five minutes to go and be irritated in peace. My job is to let her. I need to let go of wanting to insert myself in the situation. Or jumping in with an answer for the problem at hand—even if I know it in that moment. Sometimes the most effective thing you can do is stay present while that person just spools out all of their thoughts so they can naturally arrive at the conclusion on their own. It might take all your strength to not be an asshole about having known that answer all along, but again, what are you trying to win?

There's no prize for being right. There's also no punishment for being wrong. That's okay too. Know this. Be this. Tattoo this across your chest. It's the absolute truth. And it's also an essential part of not wasting your precious time and energy on conflict. Yes, even your roses smell like poo-poo-ooh. So if and when you fuck up and don't get it right, an "I was wrong, I messed up" will make anything better. That's it. Nothing else. End of story.

So You Got a Shitty Text

Nobody's perfect. People break. People yell. People say dumb, hurtful things. But that doesn't mean that you should get sucked into the nonsense. Which is why I want to share a few tips for getting through those uncomfortable interactions without making a total mess or making anyone—yourself included—feel like garbage.

Here's the scenario: You get one of those texts (or an email) that's just . . . shitty. It's rude, it's ugly, it's aggressive. And it's *long*. I'm talking like a million little boxes in a row, then one of the ones with the little arrow thing, and when you press the arrow it's like an ancient scroll unfurling down your entire screen. It's incoherent, there's typos. It's like you can feel them pounding the keyboard.

Here's what you're going to do because going in half-cocked like you actually want to right now is not gonna work out the way you think it will:

1. Write the crazy thing . . . in the notes app on your phone. Go ham.
2. Put it away for five to six hours.
3. Go back to your first response. Read it. Make some edits, some tweaks. Maybe you're more upset, maybe you're less upset. Put it away.
4. Look at it one more time before you go to bed. STILL DON'T SEND IT.
5. When you wake up in the morning, look at it one more time. Do you still feel like you want to send it? Nine times out of ten, I'm guessing you won't. Because the response you had when you were upset is different now that you've had time to process those initial feelings. You probably aren't as fired up anymore. Maybe you even see a path forward. Or understand why that person was upset in the first place.

What would have happened if you'd sent the original response? Drama. I don't know about you, but I don't have time for drama.

This simple exercise can save you so much time and energy. And if you're worried that waiting this long to respond will only make the situation worse, which is reasonable in a more personal situation, just set the boundary with them up front: "Hey, I'm hearing everything you're saying. I need some time to process this because I don't want to say anything that I might regret. I promise I'm going to write you back." Copy, paste.

The real lesson here is be a good person and be good to people. If you're not ready to do that, then put this book down and go waste your money on some shitty therapy book that you're probably not going to read. Or maybe just flip to the next chapter.

I'll Take a Karma Latte (With a Side of Humble Pie)

I've always just believed that it was common sense to be decent. To be honest. To be fair. To be kind. And I can tell you that at no point did those things make me miss out on any opportunities or succeed any less. If anything, the opposite.

There will be times in your life when you're gonna have a choice. You can either get one over on someone for an easy win, or you can do the right thing, which may not ultimately be a win in that moment. And you're going to have to ask yourself: *Is it worth blowing up this relationship over that? Is it worth blowing up my integrity?*

But here's the thing about karma: A compromise might bag you a win now, but it's never gonna end up a win in the final tally.

Take Tim. Tim is a producer. Tim is not his real name, and you'll know why in just a minute.

Many years ago, I worked on a song for an artist who we'll call Stephanie. I produced it with Tim. I was naïve and didn't understand how the music business worked, so I took a deal where I was offered a small amount of money in work-for-hire form on a song that would later go on to make millions of dollars. I fought to get the right credit after the fact but was told that that was part of "paying your dues."

Fast-forward a few years, and Tim asks me to work with an artist named John. John's music didn't connect with me, so I politely passed on the opportunity. About a year after that, John puts out a song that goes number one and eventually becomes the biggest song of the year. It also borrows a portion of the beat I made for the Stephanie song. Slightly different chords on top, but same tempo, same sound, everything.

I was so angry and had no idea what to do. Not only did Tim give me only $1,500 and no credit for a song that went on to make millions of dollars, but he used it again and gave me no credit, no money, no nothing. I didn't care about the money—it was the principle. He made me feel like I was invisible.

I had no other choice but to go speak to Tim's manager. I went to his office, and his receptionist told me that he was in a meeting, but the door was cracked and I could see that he wasn't doing anything so I walked right past her, pushed the door open, and yelled, "Tim took my song!"

He said, "benny, relax; I know you're upset, but you're just a kid. Tim is successful. An adult. He would never just take your song." I opened up my laptop and played him the two songs and then my version and explained all the similarities. He ran to close the door. Then he went on this whole spiel where he tried to get me to drop the issue. I was so frustrated that I just left his office.

I call Tim on the way home. I tell him that I could 100 percent prove that he took my song, but before I could even finish the sentence, he starts laughing over me. He said, "What are you gonna do about it? Sue me? I have so much more money than you, I'll just bury you in legal fees forever. And if for some miraculous reason you did win, you'd have lost all the money you would have made by being a writer on the song anyways and I'll never work with you again. So what are you gonna do?"

He wasn't wrong. I didn't have any power in that situation. In that moment, I said to myself, *Okay, that's what this guy is. And I'm always going to trust him to be like that.* Over the years I had to work with him on a handful of projects, but the second I could, I stopped working with him completely.

Tim may not have lost that week. Maybe not that month or that year. But I think Tim wronged a lot of people, and one day it did come around and bite him in the ass. It hasn't been the same for Tim ever since.

Don't be Tim.

Don't stand at that crossroads deciding whether you can take the shortcut of being a dick versus the potentially slightly longer road of being the decent person. There's only one good choice that's going to ultimately get you what you want.

Don't Believe the Hype

The final piece of not being a dick? Stay humble. No matter how good you are. Or how good you think you are. One day, some kid you never heard of will come up and be bigger and better than you. I promise. You might as well take each day as if it could be your last. Be appreciative that you made it this far. And remember what it took for you to get here.

When I was eight, I was in Lake Thoreau Pool in Reston, Virginia, telling all these other kids how many flips I could do and how long I could hold a handstand underwater. This kid named Peter looked at me and said, "benny's a bragger." Then all the other kids started chiming in saying, "Yeaaahh, benny's a bragger face." And they all started chanting in unison, "Bragger, brag-ger, brag-ger."

I felt horrible and embarrassed and decided I would never be a bragger face again.

I've never needed to. I let my work speak for itself. And also my actions. If I ever get tempted to feel myself a little too much in the moment, I remember that I'm being that annoying kid who got called bragger face for claiming he could do a handstand underwater.

No matter how great things get for you—and I know they will—no one likes a bragger face. And no one has time for someone who thinks they're better than everyone.

BUT, it *is* okay to be proud of yourself. And nice to yourself. Necessary, actually. Which is really convenient because that's what the next chapter is all about. I guess I'm getting the hang of this book thing after all.

c[redacted]er 6

Be Nice to Yourself.

It was 2008. I was twenty years old, standing at Nineteenth and Broadway outside of a cellphone store having a panic attack.

I'd gotten to a point where I'd had too much success too quickly (yes, that is a thing). I had more money than I knew what to do with (also a thing). I'd gone from being a kid making music and messing around having fun to being a source of income for a lot of people. People *relied* on me. I'd become a commodity, and everyone wanted and needed something from me.

I had a hard time trusting people's intentions and figuring out whether they were trying to make a genuine connection or just using me. I was being pulled in a ton of different directions and was having trouble finding any stability. I had no sense of schedule and said yes to everything because I didn't know how to say no. I didn't know that I didn't have to work seven days a week or that not doing things immediately didn't mean the world would end. It was work over everything, never stopping to catch my breath, never having anyone to help me take things off my plate.

I was eating takeout Chinese food and pizza for every meal, drinking too much, smoking too much weed, partying, and not sleeping. I had no room for friendships or family. I was in a terrible relationship. I was caught in an unhealthy, codependent, immature, everything-is-the-end-of-the-world toxic cycle. All I could focus on was what's next what's next what's next more more more.

Then the bottom fell out. I was bedridden. It was hard for me to walk. I believed my neck was going to fall off my shoulders if I didn't hold it on with my hand. It felt like there was a bonfire on the top of my head. I forgot how to swallow. I didn't leave the house for weeks at a time. I was crawling out of my own skin. For like six months.

But one day I looked in the mirror and was like, *Dude, what are you doing? You're twenty years old—you can't even legally get a beer. It's not gonna all go away if you catch your breath. You can't be one of those guys who looks around at sixty years old, realizing you built a life with no one in it. You could be doing* anything *you want. Get your life together.* So I did.

I hired an assistant because I had been doing everything on my own and couldn't do that anymore. Then I made a list of all the things that help me clear my head and make me feel balanced and did more of that every day. Like waking up at a regular time. Like moving my body and walking. Like cooking meals for myself. Like setting aside time to be with my family. Like starting cognitive behavioral therapy. The more I did those things, the less I did of the stuff that was making me feel terrible.

It's easy to get all excited about the Career leg of your stool. That's where the juicy stuff is—money, fame, success. We spent the entire last chapter talking about how to make the Relationship leg nice and strong because you can't have that one wobbling around and expect to make it to all that juiciness. Well, that leaves one more leg. Us. Ourselves. Our physical and mental health. Our sense of purpose. Our why. Our reasons for getting back up after life wipes the floor with us. Then waking up the next morning and giving the world hell.

If that leg falls apart, you won't necessarily be on your ass right away. Some people spend the better part of their lives hobbling along without it intact and making up the difference with things like sex. Drugs. Delusion. Borderline personality disorders. Usually all of the above. But one day—and you don't get to know when—it all falls apart. And I don't recommend that. So do yourself a favor and while you're building this new dream life, be sure that you're investing in you, too.

Make a Routine

When I hit rock bottom, I knew I needed structure in my life. It couldn't just be wake up whenever, work whenever, sleep whenever, repeat. Not only would work take over every minute of my life if I let it, but I also wasn't doing any of the things that made me feel good. Or like a human being meeting my basic human needs in order to, at a minimum, function. So I slowly made myself a little routine. And by the time I moved to Los Angeles when I was twenty-seven, it had really taken shape because I had grown up a little and was ready to give my life order. I've basically been sticking to it ever since.

Here's what it looks like:

Wake-up time: Consistency is key. For me, it's around 6:30 a.m., no matter what time I go to bed the night before because that's when my body naturally wakes up.

Vibe set: Usually putting on some music, something ambient like jazz or instrumentals—nothing with words or structure that my brain wants to focus on. Just a little something woozy to wake up to and maybe feel inspired by.

Touch grass: I let my dogs out, say hey to the sun, and give thanks that we all lived to see another day.

Move: I work out in the morning, so I'm up and moving before things get too crazy. If I'm in New York, I'll walk to and from the gym. In LA, I'll walk for hours around my neighborhood. That's usually when I do all my phone calls and answer texts. I do my best to answer texts twice a day and that's it. (I don't have email because, for me, it's only for spam and people who don't know how to call or text me.)

Walking is the key to evening out my spirit and soul. Anyone who lives in the LA area has seen me wandering around. I'm not a medical expert, but I'm pretty sure walking is the key to *everyone* feeling 200 percent better.

I'm not saying you have to run a New York City marathon every day, but ten thousand steps is a good goal. There's nothing easier—your phone automatically keeps track of your steps, and you'll start to realize all the moments of your day when you could be walking. I have a rule that any time I'm on the phone, I have to stand up and start moving. If you're on a call for forty-five minutes, then that's forty-five minutes you can be walking around your house or your office. And if you throw in one or two walks outside on top of that, you'll hit fifteen thousand steps without even knowing it.

Work: Meetings, studio, filming, writing, etc.

Food: Cooking checks a ton of boxes for me. It feels good because I'm not eating a bunch of garbage. It feels good because it's giving my mind a break from work and other things that creep in there and take up unnecessary space. It feels good because it's a little accomplishment, a little win. No matter how busy I am, I try to make two to three meals throughout the day. Ideally, I'll spend an hour in the morning prepping so that by the time I'm hungry, there's something ready to go. Little nori wraps with poached shrimp, potato salad with yuzu, some scrambled eggs with cottage cheese and whatever veggies I got at the farmer's market. That's another one that's always on my list: walking to the market a couple times a week to get ingredients that inspire me. It all just adds up to feeling inspired and creative and juiced for life.

Drink water: Hydrate or die. Seriously, I get anxious if I don't have water nearby. You maybe should too.

Turning it off: I do my best to end my day in time to have dinner with my family and decompress for the day.

Bed: My dream is to be in bed by 10:30/11 p.m. More often than not, the clock is after midnight. Either way, I'm helping myself wind down with a huge glass of water next to my bed so it's ready for the morning; a little lavender-chamomile sleepy essential oil blend on the inside of my wrists; an eye mask; and turning on the TV for some gentle background noise to quiet my mind, usually something Selena's watching like *Friends, Will & Grace, How I Met Your Mother.*

That's my list. My little cheat sheet. It's not some super-regimented hour-by-hour mandate, but it gives my day definition and it's got everything I need.

You only have a certain number of hours in the day. It's your choice how you spend them. Get clear on what the important things are in your life and realize that any time you spend *not* doing those things is time you're taking away from yourself.

The things I listed above are what equal success to me. A day that includes all of them, no matter how "productive" I was workwise, is a major win. What are the things that make you happiest? That make you feel your best? Could you do them every day? Or at least try? Unless you answered, "Doing drugs and fucking hookers," then I don't know about every day . . . or at all. Find healthy things. I don't mean like quinoa; I mean things that make your life positive. Things that get you excited when you wake up every morning.

I want to make sure I'm active, that I laugh, that I talk to my friends and family, that I eat dinner with my wife. Even the food I eat is balanced. I can't eat heavy meals during the day because I'll want to sink into the couch and watch *Superbad* instead of doing all the things I need to do. But if I eat little snacks here and there and keep my meals light and healthy, I'm bouncing off the walls and feeling good. I'm not a dietitian; I'm just a man who's barely five feet tall and has curly hair.

That balance also includes knowing when to turn it off. There couldn't be a better time for me to be writing this section of the book. I'm currently horizontal on a couch with my leg dangling over the arm, and I just found a piece of popcorn that was lodged between the cushions. Which I ate.

I work *hard*. I work like I've never done a thing in my life and I'm running out of time. Like I'm an intern with a dream whose big break is getting coffee for people. But I also know how to dial it back. Because we all need to recharge. That's *actually* what's going to keep you sane. Not to mention help you do better work during the times that you're on.

Give yourself little pressure release valves throughout your day. That could be at night when you finish a long day. That could be every time you check something off your to-do list. Both the small everyday tasks and the really big lifts. Give yourself a treat. Take a break. Maybe not fly to Hawaii—although, by all means—but take a load off. Go for a walk. Make yourself a snack. Hug your partner. If they're anything like mine, it's better than Xanax. Stay in bed all weekend eating sour candies and getting high. You earned it. You're allowed to because I'm telling you that you are. I'm fully certified in being a workaholic but I'm also a fully certified lazy sack of shit sometimes. Listen to your professionals.

You'll know you've got your work-treat balance right when you're having fun. Because if you're not having fun, then what are you doing it all for? My friend Jake once said to me, "You make it seem like you're always having a good time and doing nothing—when does the real work get done? Are you waking up in the middle of the night to do it, when no one's looking?" The thing is, I'm always doing the work. First of all, because there's no such thing as *not* doing it. I have to do it, and I have to make it perfect. But I'm also really good at compartmentalizing. Work is work, life is life. Yeah, things occasionally get stressful, but what am I gonna do, sit here and stress out about it or just get it all done? What's my other option? Live a shitty life? Not on the menu. I do what I need to do, take breaks when I need breaks, and move on.

The secret ingredient of all of this is the small tasks. The little accomplishments I can check off my list and feel like I've gotten a win. Hanging out with my dogs. Going for a walk. Drinking water.

When I'm doing seven million things at once—especially big things that take a while to finish—it sometimes feels like I'm not getting anything done at all, and my days blur together. But when I have these simple things that I can do in barely any time, it's such an easy, satisfying *aaaaahhh.* (In the deep breath way, not the screaming way.) It helps keep the wheels on.

Does everything on this schedule get done every day and every night? No. Do I beat myself up if it doesn't? No. Do I make a conscious effort to try to do it? Yes. And if it doesn't happen today, there's always tomorrow. I'm not asking you to become a new person right away. I *am* asking you to just try. A little bit. Every day. And if you don't want to, then don't do it. It's not gonna change my life. But you bought this book and are reading it now, so I'm guessing you care, at least a little bit.

Make a List

Lists are the magic sauce of your get-your-life-right plan. They remind you of things you need to do and that you want to do. It's like putting little goalposts everywhere to set yourself up for micro wins. I'm pretty sure someone somewhere conducted a study comparing crossing things off a list and cocaine and the list was hands-down a better high.

I make multiple lists in my notes app every single day. I'm so insane about making lists that I have lists about other lists I have to make.

Here are a few daily lists that I keep:

Things I want to cook or eat
Groceries to buy
People to call back (professional and personal—
anyone need a little check-in?)

Gift ideas for people based on things I know they like
Work deadlines
Meetings to schedule
Podcasts to listen to
Trips to plan
Books to read
TV shows to watch
Dreams I'm investing in
Date-night plans
Restaurants to try
Restaurants I like that I always forget
Events or parties I want to plan
Holidays to plan
Stuff I didn't get to yesterday
Stuff I need to schedule for tomorrow, next week, next month

Just making that list got me a little buzzed.
I highly recommend you try it.

Learn to Say No

No is the most powerful word that exists.

I used to think saying no made you an asshole and that saying yes was the "nice" thing to do. I thought I had to agree to anything anyone asked and then just let them down later. If at all.

I learned that the truth will set you free, and that includes throwing out a big fat NO every now and then. It's called having boundaries, which is basically telling people to fuck off in the nicest way possible so that you don't become a shell of a person having a nervous breakdown on Nineteenth Street.

It's natural to think that if you don't give people what they want, you're gonna wind up losing your place in line. The thing is, the only surefire way that you lose it all is if you don't keep any of it for yourself. Saying no is your extended warranty for your stool. Or maybe it's the superglue that holds it all together so it doesn't fall apart in the first place. Either way, it's what makes sure you don't wind up on the floor.

When I was twenty years old, I was finishing up Britney Spears's album *Circus* in Los Angeles. My girlfriend at the time had gone back to London to renew her visa. After about three months, she finally got a temporary travel visa and then had some work in New York, where I wanted to meet up with her because I hadn't seen her that entire time, and when you're a kid, three months might as well be thirty years. I bought a plane ticket for the next flight out (this was before I decided I'd never do that again).

When I mentioned the trip to the higher-ups, they told me that if I left, I wouldn't get any credit on any of the songs I was working on. "You have to be here from the start until the end."

It was bullshit. I'd been working on these songs for six months already. I told him that leaving for a day or two shouldn't affect that.

He said he didn't care and that's not how it works.

Like I said, I was only twenty. I hadn't been in rooms with people like Britney Spears. It was all new to me. Was this protocol? Was he right? Was I wrong? I was petrified of losing what felt like a once-in-a-lifetime opportunity. And normally, I'd go along with what people told me.

But remember, this was post–scraping myself off rock bottom. For the past year, it had become so important to me to feed every part of my life. And not going would mean not feeding my relationship with my partner, who I loved.

So I said to him, "I'm gonna go to New York City, and I'm gonna see my girlfriend. You're not going to push me into a corner and bully me. If you wanna take me off the songs for leaving for two days, you can. I made these songs, and I can make others, too. Do whatever the fuck you want." And I walked out of the room.

He was stunned. And clearly bluffing. I left and went to see my girlfriend, came back to finish the songs, and he never brought it up again.

I had no other choice *but* to learn how to create boundaries. It took me wanting to throw myself off a building, like actually going insane, to get to this point. But you don't need to get to that place in order to realize this.

You don't need to be an asshole about it, either; there's a perfectly nice way to say no.

"I need to step away from our work together for a moment. Trust me that I know we can hit our deadlines and do the best work we can do in the time we have."

"Hey, thanks so much for the opportunity, but that doesn't really resonate with me, and I'd rather someone who's super passionate about it got the chance."

"I'm super busy right now and not going to be able to give this project the attention it deserves."

"Thanks for including me, but I'm gonna sit this one out. Hit me up another time."

I'd argue that you're being a bigger asshole by saying yes to someone and then only being half in it because you don't really care. Or saying yes and then having to juggle that thing with seven million other things and none of them get your full attention.

There will be an adjustment period when saying no might make you uncomfortable. Get okay with the possibility that you might miss out on things. But in the long run, it's a wash because you're making more space for yourself. Which means you're setting yourself up for not just more opportunities, but the ones you actually want.

Rip off the Band-Aid. Say no. Keep moving. Trust me, it'll work out.

Delegate and Let Go

We're programmed to believe that working hard means doing the most. That we need to be running ourselves into the ground, working three phone lines and two computer screens at once, downing six shots of espresso, and having heart palpitations. I'm all for outworking the competition, but a really good entrepreneur never lets it get to that point. At least not most of the time. They realize their time is worth more than micromanaging situations and getting in the weeds with tasks that don't require their expertise when there are plenty of people who could do it just as well.

The saying "It takes a village" couldn't ring more true in my life. I've done a lot of things, but I haven't done any of them without help. The fact is, we can't do it all by ourselves. And if you're serious about getting to that next level, then you have to think about building a team to support you and be willing to let go of some of the stuff on your plate.

Do I know how to do laundry? Yes. But if I could be finishing a script for a TV show that's being shot in three days or remastering an album or checking off any of the literal hundreds of things on my to-do list that only I can do, then I'm gonna do that and find someone who can help me with the laundry.

That's actually not such a great example because I'm so obsessive-compulsive that if somebody else does my laundry, I still have to unfold and refold everything, then color-coordinate it by category. We all have our limits. But for real, you can't do it all. I tried. I thought I was too smart to let an assistant handle booking a few appointments. Or have an assistant in the first place. It sucked. Now, whenever I'm feeling overwhelmed and like I can't come up for air because I'm too busy, the first question I ask myself is, "Am I delegating enough? Or is my own ego saying that nothing will get done unless I do it getting in the way?" Most of the time the solution is getting my head out of my butt and asking for help.

I don't care how incredible and smart and talented you are. We've already covered how you only have so many hours in the day—why not spend most of them on the things that are really high on your list of goals instead of killing yourself over making sure that there aren't any dust bunnies under your sofa or scheduling next year's colonoscopy or adding things to your calendar. Or any of the other things that someone could just as easily do for you, if you budgeted for it.

Whenever someone tells me that they're looking for an assistant or someone to help them out in some way, I always ask them why they think they need that person. Their answer should always be: "Because I have so many things going on that I can't get to certain tasks that I need to do throughout my day." Or "I can't spend the time that I want on the things that are really important to me because I'm too busy with everyday-life kind of stuff."

Look over your daily to-do list. See anything on there that someone else could do 70 percent as well as you and would therefore give you more time to get the important things done? Offload it.

Another important part of delegating is accepting that you're delegating. A lot of people say they're ready to delegate, but they're not. So they micromanage every situation and wind up not teaching the person they're delegating to. Then they have to fix all kinds of problems and end up with double the amount of work they would have been doing before they had an assistant.

There will be mistakes as you and your team learn each other's patterns and behaviors. That's okay. If both of you do your job correctly, those will be fewer and farther between. A great assistant or support person doesn't wait for you to ask them to do something—they anticipate. Borderline read your mind. But that only comes from letting them try—even if that means they mess up every once in a while. You could have the best support network in the world, but if you suck at delegating, they're going to suck too. It's time to let go.

Get Out of Your Head

Everyone gets in their head sometimes.

Anyone who says they don't is messing with you. Or a sociopath.

When I was a kid, I would go to my mom and say things like, "The Thomas family is perfect. They never fight; everything's always right with them." And my mom would say, "They have their own problems. Everyone has their own problems." She's right.

The same idea applies here. Even the most successful people doubt themselves. I remember sitting with Ed Sheeran after the final show of his "÷" tour, at that time the highest-grossing tour for a single artist ever. We're talking almost nine million tickets, 260 shows. We're having a beer and he looks at me and says "I guess this is it. It's all downhill from here. I'll never be able to do this again."

In my case, I have anxiety. I just do. It's in my bones. No matter how chill I seem or how much my life seems together, I still find myself worrying about things I can't control, like cancer. Or having a heart attack in my sleep. All because too many good things might be happening. When I put out two albums that didn't work, I heard that little voice going, *Am I ever going to put out another album?* The same goes for Selena. And my friend Ed, and pretty much every other person who does what they do really well. Sometimes that voice sounds like, *This idea isn't good enough.* It sounds like, I'm *not good enough.* It sounds like, *People don't believe in me.* It sounds like, *Why me?* It sounds like, *It's just a matter of time before this all goes away.* It also sounds like, *I'm doing something that hasn't been done yet, so I have no idea whether or not it's gonna work.*

It makes sense—when you're constantly pushing yourself, there are going to be moments where you're second-guessing in all kinds of ways. That's how you know that you, the human being, are still in there. And yeah, maybe a little bit of childhood trauma too. But basically, you're still the same person who, at some point in your life, wasn't anywhere near having these things happen. Maybe even a person who, just a few chapters ago, I had to grab by the shoulders and tell to shut up so you could get past these thoughts and just get started. So be nice to yourself.

That voice is never going to disappear completely. But it's crucial that you figure out how to turn down the volume. Not because talking shit to your own self is unhealthy and doesn't feel good—although, yeah, that too—but because that voice is holding you back. That voice is keeping you from taking risks. No risks, no reward. In my head, that voice casually passes through from time to time, but it's never for long and it's never made me second-guess myself. Because of that, I've always dived headfirst into things like an idiot. And so I've failed. A lot. Maybe more than most people. But it also means I've succeeded more, too. Not getting stuck in your head is as close as it gets to having a superpower. So we have to figure out a way for you to get back out if and when you do.

When I signed my first publishing deal at eighteen, it was like I forgot how to make music. It was like literally overnight, everything I made sucked. I called my mom crying and told her that I didn't know how to do it anymore. It all felt like a ruse. Like I'd somehow tricked everyone into believing I was someone I'm not. I was too scared that I'd finally gotten here and I was gonna blow it. I was scared that I was going to fail (because I didn't have this book yet). But then, after a couple hours of spiraling, I realized that I needed to chill out. I needed to get back to work. And good music eventually came.

I learned that when I take my mind off what that voice is saying to me and do my best to relax, that's when the best ideas come. That's when the solutions come.

That can be little things you do throughout your day. For me, making a sandwich is like mainlining heroin because it helps my brain turn off for a second.

So does smoking a joint.

So does talking to my partner.

So does hanging out with my friends.

So does going for a walk.

So does making a list.

So does standing up and taking a step back.

Sometimes, and I'm not proud of this, it's opinion shopping. I ask a million people what they think about whatever it is I'm working on and wait to hear what I'm trying to hear. I try to not do it, but if we're being completely honest, I do.

And finally, there's just closing my eyes and breathing deeply while I slowly count to five. We don't have to call it meditation. We don't have to call it breathwork. We can just call it what it is, which is sneaking into a corner of the room and taking a second to let any anxiety or stress wash over you. A lot of times I fall asleep when I'm supposed to be just breathing because I'm basically just a baby who can fall asleep anywhere, anytime, especially in a moving vehicle past 5 p.m.

This isn't some fake New Age nonsense. This is what's actually worked for me. Don't like what I have to say about it? Listen to them:

> Self-doubt is like a droopy-eyed sloth clinging to my back. It's always there when I'm trying something new

or pushing outside my comfort zone. It's full of old "what ifs?" and "not enoughs."

I don't try to quiet it. I engage with it. If I feel self-doubt, it is because I am embracing discomfort, breaking barriers, and attempting something new. I now see it as a sign for growth. And I use it like a secret agent. It can show me everything that might trip me up, and what to be aware of in advance.

— JAY SHETTY —

Self-doubt gives me fear of failure in relationships. It makes me fearful of trying new things. It makes me retreat when I'm in large groups of people. It helps to tell myself (and sometimes others) the things I've accomplished. I remind myself of things I'm good at. But also, as I've gotten older I'm not as concerned with what other people think of me.

— SANDY LEVIN (MOM) —

Self-doubt for me is having bad writing days. If I have a bad session or write a shit song, I start to doubt if I can do it anymore. It's also hard to see the forest for the trees when you're fried and tired and overthinking. Even "Shivers" seemed like a terrible song when I first wrote it because I was in my head about it. I don't think you can ever quiet the voices. You have to be super vulnerable to be creative. I think embracing failure and embarrassment is key, and knowing you have to take risks. With songwriting, you have to take big swings to get a big hit, but big swings also have big misses. And if you fall, you have to pick yourself back up and try again. That's what it's all about. I've learned nothing from success but everything from failure.

— ED SHEERAN —

I am constantly battling my own thoughts. I am uncomfortable when people talk about my achievements. I sometimes downplay them because I am my harshest critic. I struggle with perfectionism and people-pleasing. I understand that it is impossible to satisfy everyone, yet I still try. Seeking validation from others can be one of the most disheartening cycles. It's crucial to remember that you are exactly who you're meant to be. But I am human and fall into the trap of comparing myself to others. When those external unsolicited opinions from people I don't even know begin to occupy too much of my self-worth, I've learned that stepping away from social media is necessary.

What I've come to understand is that managing these internal battles takes consistent practice. It doesn't resolve overnight. First and foremost, I have to acknowledge my feelings. It's important to identify what is troubling to me and not push it aside. Accepting my emotions is a crucial step toward managing them. Next, I challenge my negative thoughts. I interrupt the pattern by asking myself if these thoughts are valid, if they're even relevant, or if I'm unnecessarily being hard on myself. More often than not, I realize that I am holding onto something that is distorted. Taking that pause helps me shift my perspective and move forward with a clearer, more grounded view.

— SELENA GOMEZ —

Self-doubt and impostor syndrome often show up for me as intense self-criticism. I've woken up and thought, *Why am I different from any other artist? Why am I special?* It starts to feel like it's all a joke and it can't be real. Why me? I feel my paintings are bad and don't live up to my heroes, and sometimes I even feel like a complete fraud. I'll say terrible things about some of my paintings when I'm working on them or when I have a critique with a friend; my wife, Shio; or a dealer.

I try to strive for a balance of both questioning and confidence at the same time, and maybe that's what creates a healthy critical mindset. If you make a lot of stuff and think it's all great, you're probably a fucking idiot. But if you think it's all terrible, you're probably either depressed or not seeing your own talent. So I guess it's about finding a middle ground.

Sometimes impostor syndrome feels like a defense mechanism for the ego. If you never question yourself, how could you be critical of your work? It's that self-questioning that helps refine what you're doing. After you've had a breakthrough moment, where you make something incredible and feel that energy, it can be tough to return to work that doesn't feel as good. You want to stay in that high moment, but I think impostor syndrome creeps in when you think everything should be great all the time.

In the past, I've gotten caught up thinking every piece I make has to be a hit, but I know that's a trap. It's more about putting in the work every day. The "hit" comes from consistent effort and practice. What I really want is to stay in that flow state, to keep moving forward without letting self-doubt hold me back.

In the moments when I look at my work and feel like, *This isn't my best. This isn't a great painting,* I try to push and remind myself to try harder. I try to "finish strong," which is one of my mantras.

Using affirmations and mantras helps me. I have notes pinned all over my studio with phrases that bring me back to a positive mindset. I have one that says, "If you put your mind to it, you can do anything." Another one is, "Portraits, do it! Don't be lame." Portraits are hard for me, so pushing myself to make them is an important way to break through that doubt. Other affirmations I use are, "Relax and have fun," and, "I am

> good enough, don't get distracted." That "distraction" is often impostor syndrome and doubt.
>
> It also helps to have people around you who are able to be both critical and supportive of your work. People who don't tear you down completely, but also don't build you up with a bunch of bullshit either. That won't be helpful in the long run because you have to acknowledge failure, or acknowledge when something doesn't have "it." It's really through failure that you learn and grow.
>
> Ultimately, painting, or any kind of creative art form, is a practice. I call it a practice because you have to go into the studio and sharpen your sword every day. Continue to push yourself to get better while acknowledging where you are in the moment. If it's a practice, then you're not done yet; you're still climbing up, striving for something great. Thinking that way helps me quiet impostor syndrome and self-doubt.
>
> **— JONAS WOOD —**

Now you have to figure out what the voices in your own head sound like and what's going to help you turn the volume down. Maybe it's cartwheels in your front yard. Maybe it's going down to your basement and standing next to the water heater while you scream at the top of your lungs for thirty seconds so you don't throw your husband through a window. Maybe you're like my mother, where nothing makes her happier than sitting on a couch and drowning herself in reality TV that is shaving off years from her life and points from her IQ. But that's how she finds her center in order to be the rock for everyone in our family. You have to find your own way of rotting on the couch and watching another episode of *Vanderpump Rules*.

The schedule you made for yourself earlier in this chapter is your get-out-of-your-head insurance. Because the more you fill your day with things that make you feel balanced and grounded, the easier it is to see what's real and what's just noise. But you also need to know what ripcord you can pull when those voices start getting a little too loud.

Occasionally, that might mean a total system override. I once was in the studio with Charli xcx and she had a full-on panic attack. Crying, hyperventilating, the whole thing. It was early in her career, about fourteen years ago, and we were at a songwriting camp, something producers will put together for a big artist making an album—think Rihanna, Beyoncé, John Legend. It's basically a high-stakes, high-intensity think tank of the best songwriters assembled under the same roof in a handful of studios for a few days, fighting it out to see who can get a song on the album. Hence, the panic attack. I went to the freezer and I grabbed a whole bunch of ice. I told Charli to hold out her hands; then I stuck a huge handful of ice in one hand, and a huge handful of ice in the other. "You can't let go of this until it fully melts," I told her.

She started freaking out because the ice was so cold and

intense and it felt like it could burn her skin, but five minutes pass, then ten. Finally, all the ice melted and there was nothing left in her hands. She wasn't anxious anymore.

They use that technique in mental institutions for patients who can't take benzos to calm down. The ice reroutes the brain to focus on regulating the nervous system instead of whatever overwhelming thoughts it's fixated on. By the time the ice is gone, you may still have that problem, but it won't feel as big as it did.

Keep that one in your back pocket. But also, know when you might need to get advice from someone who's actually licensed to give it. Which conveniently brings me to this next section.

Know When to Call In the Pros

I think I have a pretty good sense of self. I know my strengths and my limits. I know I can handle the weight of the world on my shoulders because I've been doing it for as long as I can remember. But that doesn't mean that I don't like to have a good cry while lying in my wife's lap. And it definitely doesn't mean I'm too good for therapy when I'm not able to get out of my own way.

I love therapy. If you go to most of the people in your life with a problem, they're probably going to placate you or try to make you feel better. Or try to tell you what they think you should do. But a therapist is there to give you an unbiased opinion—no matter how bad it might make you feel. And they're there to *advise* you on what's right and what's wrong and how to make the best decisions in order to further yourself in life.

I first went to therapy when I was nineteen, twenty years old and had lost my mind. I was going three times a week, if that's any indication of how rough things had gotten. Cognitive behavioral therapy helped me work through my severe anxiety and obsessive thoughts. It took a long time, but eventually I could leave the house and take my hand off my neck without worrying that it would give out. I could sleep through the night without waking up gasping for air every five minutes because I thought I was drowning. Because I didn't give up, especially during the first six months when you're basically just giving backstory to your therapist and feel like you're burning through money and time, I slowly gained control over my own life with the tools my therapist taught me. Eventually, he became someone I could go to just when I needed to talk something out. Or when I'd have little backslides. He'd have me spin this pinwheel he had in his office that would land on things like "stomachache" and have an arrow that pointed to "cancer," but then you'd lift the flap and it'd say, "Probably just ate too much for lunch." Or "eye hurts" would be "retinal displacement"/"accidentally rubbed your eye." I learned to not catastrophize. To not sweat the small stuff. To take things as they come.

I know so many people at the top of their game who still see the value of working with different kinds of experts—relationship coaches, financial coaches, spiritual coaches, business coaches, recovery coaches. I'm guessing that they're at the top of their game *because* they have the humility to say, "I can't carry all this by myself."

It's easy to convince yourself that you can solve all your own problems. But you can't. It's just impossible. Eventually you will crumble like one of those Nature Valley granola bars. We're talking a total sea of oat dust. So do the nicest thing you can do for yourself and know when to ask for help.

Have Some Gratitude

I'm thankful every day I wake up on this planet. Because I'm still here. Because I get to do what I love. With people I love. I'm so grateful that with a cocktail of determination, luck, and karma, things have worked out for me.

Does that add up to a perfect life? I have no idea. What does that even mean, anyways? What I do know is that gratitude is the easiest, most powerful way to make your life better. It helps you put importance on the right things. It helps you have a better sense of self. It helps you not get caught up in what you might have done differently. Gratitude is the kite that lifts you out of your own negative thoughts. It helps you actually *see* all the wins. Then, suddenly, you realize how many of them you really do have because they're not getting crowded out by all the noise in your own head.

Want to know what makes all those wins feel even better? When you're grateful for everything that went into you getting there in the first place. Gratitude is feeling real appreciation for what you have and who you are, versus looking at what everyone else has and thinking that, for whatever reason, they're better off than you. That's the death of gratitude, and it sure as shit is the death of joy. Social media put a stick of dynamite on that theory's back.

Right now, you're exactly where you need to be. Because you're the only you that's ever been. You're doing awesome. Just by choosing to get up today and doing *something*. Even reading this book. That's not nothing. So even when it gets really hard, I promise you that you have so much to be thankful for. Because there was a time when you had no idea where to start. When you were maybe just praying for someone to take your call. Or hire you. Or you didn't know if you'd ever be able to get to work building the life you want. Or drinking enough water so that your pee didn't smell like rancid asparagus.

So do me a favor: Pick a thing, anything, in your life that you can be grateful for right now. And give a little thanks.

Revel in the Wins

At the beginning of my career, I never took a second to enjoy the moment that was happening right in front of my eyes. I couldn't tell you how it felt the first time I heard one of my songs on the radio because I was already so focused on what was next. I literally put myself in the hospital because I was so obsessed with the rush of chasing the next goal, the next achievement, the next record.

If I was congratulated, I'd brush it off. Make it seem like nothing. Downplay it. I have no idea why. Was I embarrassed? Did I have impostor syndrome? Was I scared that if I said it out loud that it would never happen again? At one point or another, all of the above. But mostly, I took for granted that it would just keep happening.

Until it didn't. And one day, a song of mine didn't work. Then another one. Then nobody wanted any of my new songs. But just a couple years later, I was nominated for a bunch of Grammys. Here's the messed-up thing, though: It wasn't just the failure that felt scary; the winning did, too. When I started to make it again after that first big setback, the successes freaked me out even more because when you're at the top, it can feel like there's nowhere to go but down. And I didn't like the way down felt. Any time I'd have a number one song, the first thing I'd think was, *This is the last time this is ever going to happen to me.* Or, *Will I ever be able to do this again?*

I'd gotten so preoccupied with making hits and putting so much of my worth in my career that I couldn't even pause for a slice of cake or a glass of champagne without instantly thinking about the fall. I don't know about you, but if my life has gotten to a place where cake and champagne aren't doing it for me, what's the point?

I had to change my entire perspective on what winning actually looked like. I finally understood that there was more to it than just my work. There were the people I loved. There was me as an individual and all the things I was besides someone who made music. Sound familiar? Yeah, the stool.

When I started looking at my life that way, with my career as just one piece of it, then suddenly the wins and the losses didn't matter as much. Not only that, I had more inspiration. More wells to draw from. More opportunities to feel happy. I also promised myself that if I did succeed, in any sense of the word, I'd always take a second to soak it in. Really pat myself on the back. That was a huge turning point in my life.

I started buying myself a gift for every achievement I put a lot of time and work into—a song, an album, a book, a dinner party. I don't mean a car or a house, just something small that's a sentimental reminder of the journey or a moment to appreciate and celebrate it. Sometimes it's a pack of gum. Sometimes it's a sushi dinner. When "Moves like Jagger" went number one, I bought myself a vintage T-shirt with Mick's face on it. When "Eastside," my first single as an artist, went number one, I bought a house in Malibu. But it just burned down. I don't know what kind of metaphor that is, but I have no attachment to anything material so *c'est la vie*. (Ever since I got my first "big" paycheck from producing music, spent half on a diamond bracelet, went sledding on a frozen lake in my hometown, got my arm stuck in the ice, and lost that bracelet within the first six hours of owning it, it's been animals, people, and my hard drive over things from then on.)

I'll be able to hold your hand through a lot of the issues that come up for you with this book, but this one might be the most important to me.

I've taught you how to overcome losses, but you have to learn how to win, too. I've talked about this with so many athletes, producers, actors, musicians, directors, teachers, and parents, and they all say the same thing: It's a big responsibility to be at the top or to finally get where you've been working to be. It's something that you've wanted for so long and then you're finally there and for some reason, it doesn't feel great. Sometimes that's because you've been running on adrenaline this whole time, getting high from the thrill of the chase. Then, when it's done, there's this crash. And it feels like the point might never have been about getting that thing in the first place. Don't play that game with yourself. You wanted this. You worked for it. You got it.

Sometimes that feeling comes because you're too busy thinking about what comes next. Or this accomplishment doesn't seem big enough compared to what you want to go on and do. Or it feels like all you can do is go inward and doubt. Don't do that either. You know by now to have a little gratitude. And how to get out of your head.

This book's almost over and you've just unlocked the biggest lesson that I want you to take away from all of this: If you win, have fun. Celebrate. Don't let that achievement define you by any means, but take a second and *relax.*

Whoa, that's crazy—I think that's what the next chapter is actually called.

Writing a book is kinda tight.

c[redacted]er

7

Relax.

(There's Always Tomorrow.)

All right, you've made it this far. You have a little toolbox you can carry everywhere you go. Anytime you get stressed out or you need advice or you don't know what to do, you're gonna open it up and you're gonna find the right wrench or the right screwdriver or the right hammer or I guess that's all I can think of that would be in a toolbox, but you know what I'm talking about.

I can't promise you shit. Because the hard work is on you. All I can do is give you those tools. If you leave them at home, that's not my fault. But if you do decide to carry them around (I know I should have bailed on this metaphor but we're way too deep into it now, sorry), then you got this. Now it's time to put it all into practice . . . and then let it ride.

Whenever I go to Las Vegas, at the end of my trip, I always make one last bet with all of my winnings. I put it all on black or all on red. If I win, I win. If I lose, I lose. Fifty percent of the time it's gonna work out. I'll take those odds. It's all house money anyway because I have my integrity. I'm not sure that's a good metaphor either. I don't really gamble that much. Or apparently use metaphors. But I do know one thing: After I ran out of my room naked at five years old during my mom's dinner party and told her that I was going to be the biggest artist in the world, I never looked back.

I was never trained classically. I don't know how to read music. I didn't grow up with a great model for healthy relationships. I had no connections. I don't look like an Abercrombie & Fitch model. But I've always trusted my gut. I've always bet on myself. I've always aimed high. I've always worked hard. I've never let failure define me. I've always believed that you don't have to be a schmuck to be incredibly successful at something. And that it's much cooler to be nice and care for people.

I can tell you that if you do those things, then it's gonna work out.

So close this book.

Stop listening to the voices telling you that you can't do whatever you want.

Dream the biggest dream you can. Then live like it's real. Because it already is.

Buckle up for failure. But also, fuck failure and the way you used to think about it. Like it's a missed opportunity. Or a closed door. Or a death sentence. It's just one more crucial step toward getting what you want. Especially if you're not an asshole.

Don't be an asshole. To yourself or anybody else.

And when things get hard—because they will—just remember that you're a speck on another speck on another speck that nobody's ever gonna remember. So relax. There's always tomorrow.

Acknowledgments

Thank you so much to M boogs, D boogs, J boogs, Evi, Lucas, Cora, Rio, Anika, Michael, Nana, Poppa, Mandy, Gracie, Brian, Rachel, Andrew, Zvi, Sarah, Stuart, Simon & Schuster, Doug, Carla, Reid . . . and most importantly my wife, who is always there for me and acts as my rock, my shield, and my light and when I feel like I can't keep going, picks me up, dusts me off, and makes me feel like anything is possible. I also want to thank all of my mentors, mentees, collaborators, and frankly any of my haters who told me I wouldn't make it. You were just fuel for the fire. Fuck failure . . . keep going . . . never give up.

About the Author

benny blanco is a record producer, songwriter, artist, actor, record executive, and the bestselling author of the cookbook *Open Wide*. blanco has contributed to the sale of hundreds of millions of albums worldwide through his work with artists including Ed Sheeran, SZA, Justin Bieber, Rihanna, Katy Perry, the Weeknd, Maroon 5, Juice WRLD, Sia, and many more. His two albums as an artist—*Friends Keep Secrets* and *Friends Keep Secrets 2*—have been streamed more than 11 billion times to date and have spawned multiple multiplatinum hits. blanco made his TV debut playing a fictionalized version of himself on the FXX series *Dave* with Lil Dicky, which has become the No. 1 comedy on FX and FXX. His most recent album with his wife, Selena Gomez, *I Said I Love You First*, came out in 2025. blanco's podcast with best friends Dave Burd, aka Lil Dicky, and Dave's wife, Kristin Batalucco, *Friends Keep Secrets*, debuted in early 2026 to widespread acclaim.